THE GUIDE TO BIDDING, BUYING, BARGAINING, SELLING, EXHIBITING, & MAKING A PROFIT

Auction!

BY WILLIAM C. KETCHUM, Jr.

Sterling Publishing Co., Inc.   New York

Oak Tree Press Co., Ltd London & Sydney

Acknowledgments

Douglas P. Bilodeau, South Deerfield, Mass.
Barridoff Galleries, Portland, Maine
C. B. Charles, Pontiac, Michigan
Christie's, New York, New York
R. W. Dewees, Kansas City, Missouri
Douglas Galleries, South Deerfield, Mass.
William Doyle Galleries, New York, New York
Nancy Druckman, New York, New York
Robert Elowitch, Portland, Maine
Col. K. R. French, Armonk, New York
Jim Graham, Inc., North Palm Beach, Florida
Grace Lichtensteigner, Decatur, Indiana
Harvey McGray, Lincoln, Nebraska
Thierry Millerand, New York, New York
Morton's Auction Gallery, New Orleans, La.
National Auctioneers' Association, Lincoln, Nebraska
Bryan Oliphant, New York, New York
Phillips Galleries, New York, New York
Reppert School of Auctioneering, Decatur, Indiana
The Career Institute School of Auctioneering, Parsippany, N.J.
The Missouri Auction School, Kansas City, Missouri

And for special photography, Chun Lai, White Plains, New York

Library of Congress Cataloging in Publication Data

Ketchum, William C   1931-
    Auction! : The guide to bidding, buying,
bargaining, selling, exhibiting, and making a
profit.

    Includes index.
    1. Auctions—Handbooks, manuals, etc.
I. Title.
HF5476.K43   658.84   80-52588
ISBN 0-8069-0202-7

Oak Tree ISBN 7061-2725-0

Contents

Introduction 7

Chapter 1:
The Serious Game of "Legalized Gambling" 9

Chapter 2:
The Pre-Sale Exhibition Is a Must 17

Chapter 3:
Before You Put Your Hand Up 29

Chapter 4:
What "Sold" Means 39

Chapter 5:
How to Bid and Win 51

Chapter 6:
How to Bid When You're Not There 63

Chapter 7:
Paying Up, Packing Up and Returning "Lemons" 71

Chapter 8:
How to Make a Profit 79

Chapter 9:
Tricks of the Trade   87

Chapter 10:
How to Become a Successful Seller   99

Chapter 11:
Dealing with Dealers   109

Chapter 12:
How to Become an Auctioneer   117

Chapter 13:
Behind the Scenes at a Major Firm   129

Chapter 14:
Regional and Roving Houses   139

Chapter 15:
Discovering the European Markets   147

Chapter 16:
The Serious Game That Always Was   161

Glossary   171

Appendix   179

Index   191

Introduction

During the past ten years, the remarkable growth of the auction market in the United States and western Europe has been, without question, the dominant factor in the antiques world. Of course, collectors and noncollectors alike have been generally aware of the spread of collecting, in both antiques and the later, nonantique, collectible items. But, when an American painting ("Icebergs," by Frederic Church) sells for $2.5 million, auctions suddenly become international news.

As a consequence of this kind of exposure, people are now flooding the auction houses to buy or to turn over their possessions for sale. Many of these new auction devotees have, however, only the sketchiest idea of what an auction sale is. The perils, as well as advantages, of auction trading are only vaguely understood, at best. It is the purpose of this book to serve as a primer so that you may obtain both pleasure and profit from your visits to the auction gallery.

In the first place, when you begin to dabble in the auction market, as either buyer or seller, keep firmly fixed in your mind the simple proposition that auctions are business transactions. Whatever excitement or entertainment they may provide for you is secondary. The main purpose of auctions is to sell merchandise—for the profit of the owners of the goods and their agent or middleman, the auctioneer. In this sense, auctions differ not one whit from thousands of other mercantile establishments all across the United States.

On the other hand, there is an element of uncertainty inherent in the auction world which does not exist in the typical commercial transaction. When you walk into a food or shoe store, there is an established price for everything. In this country, at least, bargaining over this fixed price is very limited. You know what you are expected to pay.

The price at auction, to the contrary, is not fixed beforehand. True, in some cases the gallery may provide a list of written estimates as to what its employees "think" the things to be sold might bring; and there may also be reserves or minimum prices on which the consignor insists before he or she will let the goods be sold. But, the estimates are at best only assumptions

7

based on prior experience and at worst, wishful thinking. They don't bind the prospective purchasers. The reserves do fix a floor under the bidding, but it is only a floor—not a ceiling. Moreover, bidders aren't told what that floor is or, in most cases, even that it exists as to a specific item or group of items.

Thus, you enter into an open-ended situation where you can, in theory, buy something for much less than it is worth on the general retail market but where you can also (quite easily) pay more than that figure. How things will come out depends on a variety of factors—the interrelationships of the auctioneer, his or her client, the consignor and the various bidders who oppose both the auctioneer and each other. All these factors will be explored here from the point of view of both the prospective buyer and the seller. The chapters on selling are especially important because the few books previously published in this field have devoted themselves almost entirely to the process of *buying* at auction. They ignore the vast number of people today who are facing a decision as to whether or not they should put their family heirlooms through auction.

If you wish to sell at auction, you should understand the advantages and drawbacks beforehand because an auction sale is a gamble (though knowledge shifts the odds in your favor), and some people make better gamblers than others. Also, many of the seeming mysteries surrounding the auction game can be dispelled if you understand just how auction houses are run, what prompts them to acquire certain goods for sale and the techniques, both proper and otherwise, which they employ to obtain top prices.

Therefore, discussions of the inner workings of the auction house, the nature of the personnel employed there, how they are trained and how they evaluate and present their merchandise to the public are included. And since the superstar of the whole auction show is the auctioneer, there is a chapter devoted to the auctioneer's role and how he or she is trained. Knowledge of this profession is particularly pertinent now when more and more men and women are opting for careers as professional auctioneers.

A lot of unkind things have been said about auctions and auctioneers—mostly by people who've gotten burned through their own ignorance of the system or their own greed. Little can be done about the latter, but it is hoped that a clearer understanding of the former will help you to avoid those pitfalls within the system and to find both pleasure and profit through buying and selling at auction.

1 The Serious Game of "Legalized Gambling"

The scene is a crowded room or tent. Piles of furniture and small accessories are stacked high behind the platform on which the auctioneer stands. The handlers or clerks carry things here and there; customers' hands wave in the air as they bid. The aura is one of intense excitement, of competition, of constant drama.

Few events—in the normal course of business affairs—compare with the glamour of an auction. It is business, to be sure, but business with a difference, *for it is also a form of legalized gambling*. All those involved: the consignors who chose this uncertain way of disposing of their possessions rather than simply selling them; the auctioneer whose day's pay is pegged to the prices he can exact for the merchandise; the buyers whose fondest hope is to buy a fortune for nothing—all of them are gamblers.

Yet, interestingly enough, the auction is the only game of chance where it is possible for all the participants to win! The consignors may realize the highest prices possible at the moment, thus allowing the auctioneer to make a fat commission while, at the same time, allowing purchasers to buy their items at a price below market value. That this does happen— and rather frequently—has much to do with the nature of antiques and the prices for which they sell.

In theory, of course, the auction embodies the purest form of market situation. Here you have the item and the seller who wishes to obtain as much as possible for it. There, in the audience, sit the opposition: bidders, be they two or two hundred, who want to pay as little as possible. All that is required for action is that more than one of those present covet the item on the block. Then, each will offer what he or she feels the piece is worth (or what he or she can pay), and the price established will be the fair market value at that given time and place.

It is this situation that those who are fond of quoting auction prices as universal market prices use to substantiate their case. But, what they choose to ignore is that rules which may well apply in the auctioning of grain futures or livestock have less application to estate and household auctions. In the first place, things sold at antiques and fine arts auctions are distinctly different from the machinery, real estate or hogs disposed of at the other types of sales.

Antiques are not like shoes or hats which are readily available and replaceable through an economic system which produces and continues to produce them, and which also generally prices them. While many are not "one of a kind" items, antiques are usually sufficiently unique that a dealer or collector seeking a specific item cannot simply pick up the telephone and order it. He or she has to seek the piece out and its price will vary depending on where it can be found and how much others in that area want it (or how much its owner thinks they want it). The more uniform the item, the more likely that both parties to the bargain will be able to agree on its established value.

Tin and iron toys of the late nineteenth century are a good case in point. Since they were made in large numbers by a manufacturing process which produced more or less uniform examples, a collector can go out seeking, say a Dogpatch Band (a 1930s musical toy), knowing both that such pieces are available and that examples in good condition normally sell for a certain sum. There will be variations, of course, depending on such things as condition of the pieces; but, for the most part dealer and auction prices will be amazingly uniform.

On the other hand, when you attempt to buy an early country Queen Anne table in the original finish or a unique, hand-carved swan decoy, you stray into an essentially uncharted land. These things were not made in a factory, and no two are exactly alike; so, prognostications as to their value must, of necessity, be much more general. Such items are the bane of the auction employee's existence, particularly if he or she takes pride in establishing accurate price estimates.

There will be sales, like the Gregory Auction of Americana, which was held at Manhattan's Sotheby Parke Bernet Gallery in 1979, where practically everything exceeds the high estimates, often by thousands of dollars. It is, in fact, customary in these times of inflation and auction mania for objects sold at auction to sell above rather than below the estimates. No doubt,

Courtesy Sotheby Parke Bernet

the auctioneer's twinge of regret at guessing wrongly is quickly forgotten in the joy of obtaining an even higher price than he thought possible!

Moreover, there are reasons other than the nature of the object to be offered that affect prices realized at auction. One of the more obvious is the nature of the buyers present. Why did two similar pieces of porcelain bring different prices at two separate but more or less simultaneous auctions? To find the answer, look first at the attendees. Often, you will discover that there were present at Auction No. 1 several important collectors and dealers in china. A similar group of competitors was absent at Auction No. 2, hence a lower price was realized for a comparable example.

For years, wily dealers and collectors sought out obscure auctions where they could "hide" from their competitors and get a good buy. This technique sometimes still works, particularly when you are dealing with small, rural auctions which are advertised only in local papers. However, the likelihood of making a killing this way is getting more remote. The increasingly common use of absentee bidding techniques (see chapter 6), coupled with the proliferation of periodicals such as the *Newtown* (Connecticut) *Bee* and *The Ohio Antiques Review*, which advertise auctions on a national basis at modest rates to the auctioneer, makes it less and less likely that a really good auction will fail to attract attention, no matter where it is located.

Another factor that may arbitrarily influence the auction price is the skill, knowledge and desire of the auctioneer who is conducting the sale. Some callers are simply better at their trade than others. So much of the auction game has to do with emotional reactions, and the skillful auctioneer can sense the mood of his audience and direct it to his own profit. Timing can be critical. Douglas Bilodeau, a well-known New England auctioneer, stresses how important the day's first sale can be, noting that, "Often the first item offered for sale sets the pace of the auction for quite a while."

"Woman Bathing" by Mary Cassatt (opposite) brought $72,000 at Sotheby Parke Bernet, setting a new auction record for any print by a woman artist. As you shall see, there are many factors affecting the prices realized at art auctions, only one of which is quality of the art.

A top auctioneer knows his buyers, their likes, their dislikes and their rivals. He plays on their desires and on their hostility to other bidders present to create bidding battles from which he and his consignors benefit. Like the huckster or salesperson, he can convince people that something is what it is not, that an ordinary hack oil painting is a work of art, that an old chair is in a style that is about to undergo an intensive and profitable revival. To an observer it may seem that this is done effortlessly and without thought. Far from it. The knowledgeable auctioneer has worked long at this trade and has prepared carefully for each sale.

A less experienced or less talented auctioneer can actually depress the prices of what he sells. If he does not know his merchandise, he lets valuable pieces slip quietly into the hands of wise collectors and dealers without alerting other possible competitors to their significance. If he does not know how to arrange the auction schedule, he sells good things too early or too late when they will neither bring top prices nor serve, as they should, to stimulate further buying.

Auction buffs recognize other situations which may have a bearing on the prices realized at auction. Some of these are obvious. Weather can be a big factor, particularly in rural areas where snowstorms or heavy rains may prevent the arrival of buyers from distant cities. You should, in this context, keep in mind that a full auction house is itself no guarantor of a successful sale. A large portion of every audience (particularly, where you don't have to buy a catalog to gain admission) is composed of spectators or those who will bid only rarely and in low figures. Those who will drive 400 miles to an auction are the serious bidders, and if they are absent due to a storm, it can have a devastating effect on prices.

Also, as we will see later, the nature of the sale and how it is advertised can be crucial. Every competent auctioneer strives to include in each auction things which will bring out the buyers, items from the estate of a famous collector or public personality or objects in themselves notorious (such as the much publicized "Bonnie and Clyde" death car). Such things may or may not have much intrinsic value, but they draw crowds; and the prices realized for them influence all prices in the sale.

Auction timing also can be important. It is no accident that the New York City auction season terminates in late June and does not resume until September. The "big" buyers, retail and wholesale, are out of the city for the summer. And, as you might suspect, it is during these warm months that the country auctioneers bring out their best pieces and hold their largest sales, hoping to lure the dollars of tourists and summer residents. The smart buyer, of course, reverses the process, buying in rural areas during the winter and in the city during the summer.

It should be pointed out, though, that like so many of the old rules, this one is subject to more and more exceptions. With the booming interest in antiques and art for investment, country auction houses are learning that they can sell anytime and anywhere. All they need is the "merch."

On the other hand, it is still a good idea to seek out auction buys in places where prices for specific items (as opposed to prices in general) are likely to be lower. Dealers in bronzes, for example, know that the New York market is no place to buy. Rural New England, on the other hand, can prove profitable. A French *animalier*'s bronze figure, lost among quilts and country furniture, will seldom realize its full value at a country sale. Local preferences definitely do affect auction values, particularly in the smaller auctions which are less likely to get a big influx of dealers or absentee bids.

Courtesy Chun Y. Lai

This is an exterior view of a country auction gallery in New York State. Note the traditional food and the American flag. Summer is busy season for these rural auction houses and "dry" season for city houses.

All of these factors go into making prices and differences in prices. At the top of the pricing scale is the so-called "world record price," a feather in the cap of any gallery which can boast of one. Initially, the term was applied exclusively to paintings and sculpture where detailed sales records of major artists have been maintained for years. Thus, the highest price realized at auction for a Rembrandt would become the "world record price" and a goal to shoot for.

With the proliferation of auction houses we now have "American records," "continental records" and even house records, i.e., the highest figure realized for a certain artist's work at a particular gallery. Moreover, records are now being kept of the most spent for a Philadelphia Chippendale highboy, for a piece of Georgian silver or even a tin toy (no joke—one toy recently went for $25,000).

Such arithmetical diligence is not without its rewards. In the first instance, being able to boast of having sold a particular artist's work for a higher price than ever before obtained is beneficial to a gallery both in general and in attracting further consignments of similar material. Moreover, the "world record" piece becomes, itself, a stimulus to higher prices. It is well known that a firm which sold a painting by a particular artist for a top figure, and then obtained more work by the same painter, will actively promote these pieces by comparing them (price-wise) to the previously sold example. The gallery contacts the underbidders on the record painting and sends out representatives armed with slides of the coming attractions in an effort to convince the previously unlucky bidders that they should seek these new and choice examples, which certainly will bring even more than the "world record" price!

Surprised at such ploys? That's "show biz!" A great deal of the contemporary auction scene has much more to do with promotion and show business than with the traditional concept of the country house sale.

2 The Pre-Sale Exhibition Is a Must

The first step in the auction process is the exhibition or "viewing" of the merchandise to be sold. When and how this is held varies greatly depending upon the quality of the sale and the auctioneer's whim.

Larger galleries regard the exhibition as being almost as important as the auction itself, and they prepare lavishly for it. Pieces to be sold are set up in a large room or series of rooms with each example numbered to correspond to a catalog description. In some cases, further descriptive material is affixed to the object or placed on a nearby wall. In the top houses, such as Sotheby Parke Bernet, Christie's and Phillips there is a calculated effort to create a museum-like setting and to furnish each major example with a background and a history or provenance which will enhance its importance in the eyes of potential buyers.

Viewings of this sort are prepared for and announced well in advance and generally extend over a period of one to five full working days. In nearly all cases, they are open to the general public without charge; though, occasionally, benefit exhibitions are held with admissions earmarked for a charity. There are also a limited number of private viewings where admission is by invitation only. Receiving an invitation to one of these depends primarily on your purchasing "track record," social connections or friendship with a staff member. In a sense, such exhibitions are really social events and a way for the auction house to gain favor with well-to-do clients and potential clients. You lose nothing by not being present for the private opening since a day or two later you, too, will be able to see and evaluate the consignments.

The typical viewing that precedes a small-town auction is

quite different from what we have just described. Usually, the public is allowed in on the day prior to the sale; but it is in no way unusual for the exhibition to be open for only an hour or two immediately prior to the auction itself. Moreover, conditions under which the merchandise may be seen vary greatly.

Some large regional firms such as Skinner's in Bolton, Massachusetts, and Bourne's in Hyannis Port, set up their exhibitions in a manner not unlike that seen in the big city galleries. On the other hand, the typical small-town auctioneer usually has neither the time nor the space for such a display. As one anonymous Pennsylvania auctioneer put it, "I'm running three auctions a month out of this place, and I've got stuff coming in here all the time. I'm lucky if I can keep the things I'm selling today separate from all the rest. Don't ask me to 'fancy it all up' for you. Besides, there may be some good stuff in there that I've overlooked. You might just find it in one of those boxes or piles."

So, at a small auction house you may find your "view" somewhat obstructed, to say the least. At some exhibitions, the only way you can see everything is to dig—drag the boxes and pieces of furniture in front out of the way so that you can get in to see what is behind them. With things piled six feet high and ten feet deep, it presents a real challenge and even some risk. Small wonder that so many country auction halls have signs advising that the management is not responsible for injuries occurring on the premises (though the actual question of responsibility is one that is governed by the laws of negligence and may differ from state to state).

And, of course, in such circumstances there is seldom a catalog or even a numbered list of the lots to be sold. A lot is a group of items, not necessarily related, that are sold separately. But more about lots later. The stuff just sits there until the auctioneer drags it out and sells it pretty much at his whim (though you may be sure that it is seldom as haphazard a process as it may appear). Some shrewd auctioneers delight in creating the impression that they don't know their merchandise, and that, therefore, great bargains are to be found galore.

You might ask, though, at least in the case of the country auctions, why bother to attend the viewing when it's such a bother? The answer, in part, is that the legalities of the auction business, as well as the practicalities of the sale, make it impractical for you to rely on the auctioneer's description of the items being sold. Barring situations of outright misrepresentation, the house can seldom be held accountable for its descriptions and hard-sell representations, since these are regarded as mere "puffing," no different from the shoestore clerk's assurances that "These are the best sandals in the world." They aren't, of course; but you can't take them back on that ground alone. The whole thing is summed up very nicely in a portion of Christie's Warranty, which appears in each sale catalog:

> All statements in the catalogue, advertisements and brochures of sale, and all statements made at the sale or preview are statements of opinion and are not to be relied upon as affirmations, assumptions of liability, representations or warranties concerning any lot sold hereunder and intending purchasers must satisfy themselves by inspection or otherwise as to the physical condition and description of any lot and as to whether or not it has been repaired or restored. The Seller and Christie's do not make or give, nor has any person in the employ of Christie's any authority to make or give, any representation or warranty.

Remarkably similar provisions appear in sales catalogs issued by many other firms in the field including Sotheby Parke Bernet, C. B. Charles of Pontiac, Michigan, and Phillips.

Prospective bidders confronted with such language often rail against the auction houses, claiming that it's "unfair" for the auctioneers to so insulate themselves and that they, the prospective buyers, are being taken advantage of. Is this really the case? Again, barring the rare case of deliberate fraud, the auction is a business process into which both parties must enter with eyes open. The auctioneer is, in the final analysis, selling merchandise like any other salesman; he is legally obligated to do nothing more than present it to the potential customer and to refrain from making statements about it which are clearly contrary to fact. Remember that, other than the limitations imposed by reserves, the auctioneer puts no price on the goods. The buyers do that.

As a buyer, it is your responsibility to overcome the initial advantage obtained by the auctioneer through his general experience and specific observation of the consignment by learning as much as you can about what you are planning to bid on. The best way to do this is to attend the viewing. Buyers who bid on items without previously examining them have only themselves to blame if they come up with a "lemon."

Now, to the actual process of the viewing. How efficient and how valuable this will be depends largely upon your knowledge and the way in which you conduct your examination. There are viewers and viewers. Some scramble frantically through the exhibition rooms, pulling open drawers, squeezing upholstery and peering into chests as though searching for that set of sterling or pocketful of gold coins which have somehow been overlooked by the dozen or so prospectors who went first. For such people, time is of the essence; though, of course, they can't start buying before anyone else.

Other prospective bidders move leisurely from piece to piece, surveying an example from afar, observing it more closely from several angles, then handling it, perhaps, but always with care and attention. Observation is the key. It is so easy for all of us to look and not to see, and seeing is the name of the game.

True seeing, as opposed to just looking at things, is based on prior knowledge. We do not see and understand what we have no experience with. Hence, the cardinal rule at auction must be, DON'T BUY WHAT YOU DON'T KNOW! It is not enough simply to attend an exhibition. You must also know what to look for.

For example, suppose you're a furniture buyer in need of a table. You should, of course, examine those on display with thoroughness. But, what will you look for? If your knowledge of the furniture field does not extend beyond a recognition that formica table tops are not customary on seventeenth century tavern tables, you are apt to be looking for rather basic things. Does the piece have four legs and do they all match? Does it have both leaves and a functioning drawer? Now, these are important requirements to be sure, but if the piece is cataloged with an estimate of $1,500–2,000, and you are willing to bid that, then, perhaps, you should know a bit more about old tables.

If you were a furniture dealer or serious collector, you would approach the piece in quite a different way—informed and confident—a way worth observing.

You would be familiar with styles and periods, with older construction methods and materials. Perhaps most important, you would have handled hundreds of other old tables. You'd approach your job with an air of familiarity and a knowledge of what to look for.

Observing the table from several angles to get a feeling of its general form, you'd then turn it over and examine the underside of the top to see if the natural discoloration caused by age was uniform throughout. Light spots on exposed surface areas or a coat of paint (tabletop undersides, of course, normally were not painted) will lead you to suspect that the top is not original—a common occurrence with antique tables.

You would also closely examine the leaves. Does the wood grain match that of the top and does the patina (the dirt and discoloration left by years of use) seem uniform throughout?

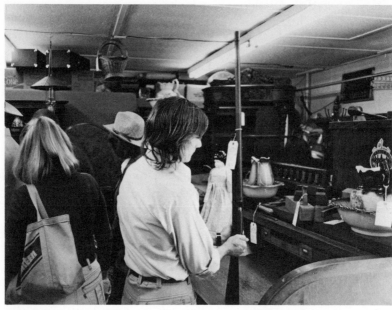

Courtesy Chun Y. Lai

A prospective bidder examines an early rifle at a pre-sale exhibition.
He is checking the breach to see if it is original and in working order.
Double-check everything!

Are the hinges of old, wrought iron, which would be right for
the period; and, even if they are, what about the screws? New
screws, just like a difference in wood grain or patina, could
mean one or more replaced leaves. What about the legs? Do
their lower extremities show the telltale saw lines that indicate
that pieces have been added to lengthen them, "ending out,"
as it's called in the trade. Knowledgeable dealers or collectors
would look for these and many other things, and their deter-
minations would influence their bidding.

Now, the kind of information you need to make such an
inspection does not come quickly. Neither this nor any other
single book can make you an instant expert, and if you wander
into an exhibition asuming that because you know that crystal
"rings" when tapped and lime glass doesn't, or that factory-
made hooked rugs come primarily in pastel colors, and that you
will be able to compete with experienced dealers and collectors
in evaluating the lots, you are just fooling yourself.

Unless you regard auctions as a form of legalized gambling

Courtesy Chun Y. Lai

When you inspect the merchandise prior to auction, do you know what to look for? You'll be up against knowledgeable dealers and collectors, so learn all you can before you bid.

and can dismiss all questions of authenticity and quality with the old saw, "I buy what I like," you are well advised to settle on a specific category of antiques to purchase—say, Depression glass or American pewter—and undertake a crash program to learn as much as you can before you put your hand up.

There are quite a few excellent sources for such information. Throughout the country adult education programs are instituting classes on antiques and collectibles. Museums and private groups are offering seminars at which leading authorities lecture. There are more books on antiques than ever before, and they are of a higher quality, reflecting new research and a broadening knowledge of our material heritage. Museums are particularly valuable, because they enable you to see early furnishings in the proper setting and provide fairly accurate information as to dates and types.

And, finally, there are the antiques shops and shows. Some dealers are more open to questions (and some know more than others), but in all cases the examples they display are priced—

a gauge of what that individual, at least, thinks something is worth. Fortunately, perhaps, even the most eager auction aficionados cannot attend more than a sale or two per week. Between times, they should be boning up on what they are planning to spend their money.

But, even if you aren't terribly knowing, if you intend to buy you must attend the viewing. That way, at least, it's possible to spot the cracks and chips in the porcelain, the ground down rims on the wine glasses and the missing drawer bottom in the bureau. The auctioneer is not obligated to tell you about such things and he may just forget to; in fact, he may not even know. Particularly at rural sales with many box lots, much of the material is never even inventoried; it is just sold.

A hunter would never head for forest or field without proper equipment. gun, bag and so on. The auction-goer, a hunter of sorts, should likewise be well equipped. First of all, if one is available, you should have a copy of the sale catalog. Nowadays, these may cost as much as a fine hardcover book at a major auction, but to dispense with one on that ground alone is being penny-wise and pound-foolish. The catalog will provide a listing of, and sometimes a brief description of, each lot to be offered,

A serious auction-goer should be well equipped. At the very least, this includes pad, pencil, lot list and/or a catalog.

along with (in some cases) illustrations of certain choice pieces. You'll need the catalog for bidding and identifying items.

You should also have a notebook in which to record comments on the material you examine (there is seldom room for this in the catalog), a pen or pencil, a flashlight (a penlight is all you need in a well-lighted gallery, but some of those country sales-rooms are so dark that you'd better bring a big three-battery spotlight), a magnifying glass and a black light (an invisible ultraviolet light). Not all of these things will necessarily be needed at a given auction. A black light, for example, would be required only if you were going to inspect paintings, glass or pottery.

Appropriately equipped and costumed (ranging from formal clothing at a New York private opening to grimy overalls for that country house sale), you sally forth. If you have a catalog, you should already have examined it to determine what you're interested in. If not, you must wander among the pieces seeking things that conform to your interests. In either case, it's best to take a quick overview of the hall to see where things are. Then examine in detail those things in which you have an interest, making careful notes as to their good and bad points and determining the top bids you are willing to make.

What you are willing to pay for a given lot depends on two things: Your financial resources and some evaluation of the object's worth. Most of us have a monetary limit beyond which we cannot go without hocking house and car. Even if you are not so restricted, recognize that there is a price you should not exceed. Where estimates are published, these provide some guide. As we shall see later on, though, estimates are at best only rough approximations of value. Often they may reflect compromises between auctioneer and consignor which have little relationship to market realities. At best, they are guide-lines. Far better is the sort of pricing knowledge in your field which is achieved by auction observation, show and shop visits and the reading of publications in the antiques field.

It may not be easy to arrive at a bidding limit, particularly if you really want a certain item; but it must be done. It is far easier to make such a determination now than it will be in the heat of battle.

Enter information as to condition and bidding limits in your notebook alongside the catalog number of the lot in question. If there's no catalog or lot list, describe the piece fully enough so that you may identify it quickly when it is put up for sale. Where a box lot is involved, you may need to describe the merchandise by its container—"green apple box with one sideboard missing."

When dealing with box lots at a country auction, however, don't assume that the one item you're buying the whole box for will necessarily be there when it is auctioned—particularly, where box contents are not enumerated. It is common practice at many viewings for the potential bidders to busy themselves "salting" a particular box for which they plan to compete. The same choice piece (which the auctioneer may have thrown in to begin with just to liven things up) may move from box to box during the hours immediately preceding the sale. Last one with his hand in the box gets the goodies!

The matter of identification is particularly important when dealing with lots containing more than one item. Catalog descriptions of such lots usually appear as a number followed by a slash and then by another number (#412/3), thus indicating Lot Number 412 consists of three objects which may or may not be related. The phrase pair or "pr." shows that the items have a relationship, as a pair of cruets. Sometimes a lot consisting of several examples loses one or more members somewhere between exhibition hall and auction block. Particularly in auctions without catalogs, it is important to have your description handy so that you may be sure that you are getting all that you saw and based your bid on.

Auction house personnel will be present at most pre-auction viewings, and they can be helpful to you in various ways. They can locate pieces which are listed in the catalog or advertised, but which you can't seem to find. They can handle fragile things and remove items from locked display cabinets so you can take a closer look, and they can provide information. But remember, the gallery can seldom be bound by what they say; they are there to boost the goods.

One of the ways gallery personnel do this is through lining up a group of potential bidders for a choice piece. Let's assume that you're a collector of cast-iron penny banks, and a good example is coming up for sale. You ask to see it. The auctioneer or gallery assistant proudly displays the piece and then remarks, most solicitously, that it appears that a bidder would have to come close to the upper estimate on this, because so-and-so (a well-known collector) has already declared that he will pay X amount. If you fall for this you will in some way indicate your willingness to better that figure. And on it goes. With luck, the gallery can have several people lined up before the auction even gets underway, all of them ready to pay a top price for the bank.

Inspect all crystalware with great care. Check to see if there are chips, cracks or repairs in the piece, as they will lower the value. Always turn piece over to its glass base. Ideally, you'll notice the proper marks of wear and tear, reflecting age. So if the base is smooth, use caution!

Most auction-goers, particularly dealers and serious collectors, aren't fools, though; this sort of thing must be done subtly. On the other hand, everyone—or almost everyone—likes to know who the opposition is; if the individual named as a prospective bidder by the house representative does bid on the piece, you wll be even more likely to believe what he says the next time around.

Once your inspection is completed, you may have a few more things to do before you tackle the bidding. In the first place, you may have a list of unanswered questions.

What about the manufacturer's mark on the teapot? It was on the base, and that's where they're usually found. What's more, it looked like a pair of crossed swords, a mark used by Meissen, one of the world's finest porcelain manufacturers. But you can't guess on something like that, especially since you may recall that other companies used similar marks. Worse yet, there are fake Meissen pieces! What to do? Back to the books!

And what about that oil painting which is cataloged only as "American Style?" You checked the lower area of the front, as well as the frame and back of the canvas (the areas where a painter's signature usually is found) and there doesn't seem to be a name. Yet, there is something very familiar about the style: the way the woman is sitting, the colors in the background, the book she is holding in her hand. Where did you see something like that before? Wasn't it in that book on American painters, and wasn't the picture credited to Ammi Phillips, a famous early painter? Again, it's back to the books. Knowledge is power and this is no time to go on hunches.

Now, of course, if the viewing immediately precedes the sale, you may not have much time for the needed research. But if there are a few days, or even a few hours available, it really pays to try and get answers to your questions—from research books, from museum people who can often be very helpful or from private experts.

You may even decide to pay one of the experts to come in and give you an opinion on a particular item. Of course, you may have the problem of his later bidding against you if yours is a real find! You probably wouldn't know his bidding tricks though, since, unless he were a real fool, he would employ an agent.

In any case, unanswered questions about lots you'd like to bid on should be resolved, whenever possible, before the bidding opens. Then, if you've done your homework well, you'll be putting something more than money where your mouth is!

3 Before You Put Your Hand Up

There was a time—and not so long ago—when auction attendance was a mandatory Saturday afternoon ritual in many small towns, just as was moviegoing in larger communities. Whole families would come, bringing granny, the kids and sometimes even the dog. There were picnic baskets, thermoses of coffee or bottles of beer and a general feeling of merrymaking, heightened by the presence of all those friends and neighbors you hadn't seen for a week—not since the last auction!

Auctions were shorter then and slower paced. The auctioneer was not only a salesman, he was supposed to be a comedian, as well. He usually knew—and was known in—the community, so individual sales often were interspersed with jokes and stories about the merchandise and its former owners. The items sold were a mixed bag, usually reflecting the breakup of a farm or disposition of a small estate, and those who bought often did so for practical reasons: to get a second tractor, to replace an old sofa with a slightly newer one or to obtain some more jars for fall canning. But, always, the assumption was that this was used merchandise and prices should reflect that fact.

Well, a lot has changed in the past decade or two. Auctions are now big business, particularly if the items offered are antiques or collectibles. Even rural sales will often bring in tens of thousands of dollars, and many of the faces in the auction hall are now those of strangers, out-of-town buyers who may have come hundreds of miles to attend.

Coffee and junk food machines have replaced the basket lunches and the Ladies' Aid sandwiches. No dogs are allowed and, often, no children, and the sales may be held on any day of the week, day or night, though Saturday and Sunday are still the preferred times.

But these changes haven't altered the basic excitement of the sale, whether it be held on a lawn, in a country Grange hall or in a large city gallery. The auction still remains a lively form of entertainment and, providing that you don't bid, one of the least expensive ones!

Time was when it wasn't that easy to find auctions, particularly in unfamiliar territory. Auctioneers were a thrifty lot, and they often announced their business with nothing more than a line or two in the local weekly and, perhaps, a few flyers slapped up on notice boards and trees in the neighborhood. You may still come upon a few rural sales in this manner, particularly the summer charity auctions so common in rural New England and the midwest. It's pretty exciting to get to such a sale and not see a face that looks like a dealer or another collector. Unfortunately, in many cases, there is a good reason for this, and it's not the lack of publicity. Most charity auctions rely on donations, and there are few people left today who are so naive as to give away Federal breakfronts or even decent Depression glass. Most of the things sold at such auctions are, accordingly, either new or junk.

It's a safe bet that any contemporary auction of any quality will be well publicized, and you will have no trouble finding it. Sometime between Wednesday and Saturday the ads will start appearing in daily papers. They will often take up a whole column with some descriptions of the choicer merchandise, occasional illustrations and the usual information as to the sale location, hours and terms of payment.

Nor is the duration between notice and sale necessarily so brief. In these days of transcontinental travel and high demand for quality antiques, major sales may be advertised months in advance in such periodicals as *Antiques Magazine, Antiques Monthly* and the *Antiques Journal.* Even more auction notices appear in regional publications like the *Tri-State Trader* and the *New York-Pennsylvania Collector.* These basically tabloid weeklies or monthlies receive a major portion of their advertising income from auction ads and may often list several dozen in a single issue, most of which will be confined to the area they service. The tabloids also frequently carry auction reviews which are brief articles on recent sales mentioning items sold and prices realized. Such stories can be helpful in choosing which auctions to attend. If a given house always seems to have good merchandise, it will probably be worth checking out.

There are other ways to find out about auctions. You can always look up the local auctioneers in the Yellow Pages and ask them what they have scheduled. Or you can ask dealers, fellow collectors and the people who staff those roadside tourist information centers. If the latter know, they will probably tell you; if the former do, they probably won't. After all, you are more potential competition, and who needs that?

But searching aside, once you have selected your auction, there are preparations to make before you arrive and eagerly raise your hand to bid. The first thing you do, of course, is to read the sale advertisement. What are the dates and hours of the exhibition? What sort of payment will the house accept? Is the sale in a hall? If outdoors, will it be held even if it rains? Is there a prepared calalog and, if so, how and where can you get it? In short, the typical auction advertisement contains a wealth of information you can use to determine if you want to attend and how you should be equipped.

The actual business of attendance at the sale would seem, at first glance, to be rather straightforward. You walk in, sit down and start bidding. Well, it can be that simple; but the sophisticated auction buff is likely to have things a bit more organized.

For the aficionado, the auction trip starts several days before at the preview. At that time you evaluate the merchandise and the competition through observation and questioning of gallery personnel. Your hour of arrival will be based, in part, on your assessment of how crowded the house will be and when you need to appear to get good seats. If you're attending a rural auction where you will carry away your purchases on the day of sale, check out the parking facilities to see how close you can park and still avoid being blocked by late arrivals. No one wants to carry a sideboard or an Oriental rug very far, but if the alternative is to wait until everyone between you and the road has left, those few extra yards of toil may be worth it.

This is also the time to prepare and review your auction "survival kit." Is there rope to tie things to the top of the car or truck? What about weather aids like suntan lotion or an umbrella for outdoor auctions, and a folding chair if no seating is furnished? Boxes and wrapping materials may also be important at those local sales where they dump everything in your lap as fast as you bid it in. And, what about food and drink? Auction advertisements often are listed as "catered." This term can cover a multitude of sins. On the one hand, it may mean the local firemen's auxiliary, serving homemade soup and great brownies. On the other, it implies leathery hot dogs and watery coffee. The knowledgeable auction-goer finds out what is being served and acts accordingly. I have known people who arrive at the sale with everything from a well-chilled white wine to an elaborate dessert. For them, the auction was a gastronomic, as well as an emotional and esthetic treat. This may be carrying it a bit far. On the other hand, auctions today will often run as long as six hours at a stretch and, particularly if what you came for is way down the list, you ought to be as well-fed and as comfortable as possible during the session. And while cases of sunstroke at summer auctions are rare, I have seen people with spectacular sunburns at the end of a long day outdoors.

Courtesy Missouri Auction School

The contents of an old hotel are being auctioned off at this "premises" sale in the South. Several auctioneers are working this out-of-doors sale where the merchandise didn't justify removal to the gallery.

Courtesy Chun Y. Lai

Select your seat early, while all others view "merch."

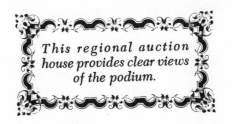

This regional auction house provides clear views of the podium.

Unless the sale is to be conducted under a canopy, it pays to
supply yourself with a protective lotion or a beach umbrella.

And always check the seating facilities when you attend the
pre-auction viewing. Most halls where sales are held are supplied with some form of seating, either benches (often back-
less) or those rickety wooden folding chairs which have a way
of collapsing under you at a critical moment. All tend to become
uncomfortable after a few hours. It pays to take along a pillow;
and, in winter, a blanket, though some halls are too hot and the
mass of auction attendees will generate enough heat to keep
you comfortable.

If the sale is outdoors rarely will seating facilities be available, so you will need to bring your own. The best, by far, is
the light aluminum and plastic folding chair. It is easy to carry
and to maneuver through crowds and takes up little space.
There are people who never take a chair to an auction, but
standing for six hours or sitting on the damp ground or a hard
wood floor (from where you usually can't see anything, anyway) isn't very practical.

Where you actually choose to sit at an auction is very much
a matter of personal taste. As a general rule, if you are there to
bid, you should be in an area where you can clearly see the
auctioneer and the lots being put up, not because you are trying
to determine their condition at that point (you have, hopefully,
already attended the viewing), but because you want to be
able to identify what you intend to bid upon. This is particularly
important at smaller sales where there is no catalog or lot list
and no numbered lots. The auctioneer simply puts something
up on the block, describes it briefly and calls for bids. Under
these circumstances, and especially if several similar items are
to be sold that day, it is most important to be sure the piece
is the one you inspected and described in your inspection notes
(see chapter 2).

Even where a catalog is available, a lot will often consist of
more than one item, and you will want to see if all the pieces
you looked at are still there. And it never hurts to have that one
last look before you start bidding. A lot of things can happen
between exhibition hall and auction block, and a missing table
leg or newly cracked mirror might cause second thoughts.

It is also, of course, extremely important that the auctioneer
be able to see you so that he may acknowledge your bids.
There are some who feel that the way to achieve high visibility
is to look "different"—to dress in a luxurious or bizarre manner.

Undoubtedly, this will attract attention, but it is not recommended. In the first place, looking as though you have money will encourage an auctioneer with larceny in his heart to use all the tricks at his command to extract your top bid. Moreover, every auction crowd has its few "kooks," angry or resentful people who will be quick to take offense at anyone different. Once you realize that one or more of these characters is running you up every time you bid (see chapter 5), you will think twice about attracting attention.

Besides, it really isn't necessary. If you are in the auctioneer's line of sight, he will see your bid. It's his business to do so. Once you have made several bids on several objects he will not only see you, he will be looking for you!

In general, there are two preferred bidders' locations. The first is "down front," several rows directly in front of the auctioneer's podium. So popular is this location that certain of the larger national and regional galleries reserve these seats and distribute them among their heavy buyers.

Even at smaller auctions it is often possible to reserve a front row seat by calling or writing in advance. Sometimes all you have to do is arrive ahead of the crowd. Of course, this may mean claiming your spot as much as two hours before the first lot is knocked down. At sales where the exhibition is held immediately prior to the auction, it is customary for the first ones in the door to take the front seats and then preview the goods.

Other than the questionable aspect of prestige, there are some good reasons for sitting down front. Being closer to the goods being sold, you can get a better look at them. The auctioneer can also get a better look at you, which may be particularly important if you are bidding in a secretive manner, such as by crooking a finger or winking (see chapter 5).

There are, however, some very good reasons for not sitting in the front row seats. In the first place, your view is extremely limited there. Without constantly turning around, you cannot see who may be bidding against you. You run the risk that no one is; that the auctioneer, seeing your vulnerability is "taking bids off the walls," as they say in the trade (see chapter 5). Moreover, you are particularly visible down front, and it is easy for anyone to run you up or to get some idea of what you are buying (perhaps, to see what markup you put on it in the shop if you are a retailer).

Accordingly, there are bidders, and a substantial number of them, who prefer other locations. One of the most favored is the back of the room. From here, assuming the space is not too large, you have a clear view of the other bidders and the lots being put up (though, how clearly you can see the lots depends upon the distance involved). Being a back-row bidder, particularly if you are standing, allows you to be seen clearly by the auctioneer who can spot your bids, yet is restrained by his knowledge that you, like himself, can see nearly all that is transpiring in the house. That you may have to do a lot of standing, however, particularly if those in the front rows are standing—or wearing tall hats—goes without saying!

Standing, in fact, is definitely preferred by some auction attendees. You will see them at every sale, prowling about the aisles and leaning against pillars. Some stand because they have bad backs, some because they feel that they may be more easily seen, and others because they do not want to be seen. By moving from spot to spot, they hope to avoid the scrutiny of those who are bidding against them or feeling curious about what they are buying. This behavior is carried to an extreme in the the case of a few bidders, the "lurkers." These souls may be found hiding behind posts, appearing only to flash a secretive bid, skulking in the corridors or rooms immediately adjacent to the auction hall, and even running in and out of the room when the things they are seeking are being put up. As eccentric as their behavior may appear, these bidders are often very serious buyers; auctioneers often know and cater to them.

Wherever you may choose to sit or to stand, the important thing is to be there when the action starts and to be ready to bid on those things in which you have an interest. This means having your catalog (where one is available), your description and comments noted at the exhibition and your list of bidding limits (see chapter 6) all within reach. Without these, you should be only a spectator when the bidding starts; which, incidentally, isn't a bad way to break into the auction game. It never hurts to spend a couple of sessions just watching the action and getting a feel for the whole auction process.

4 What "Sold" Means

Early auctioneer.

Once you attend an auction, you are made aware, however superficially, of the legal conditions under which it is held. If a catalog is available for purchase, somewhere within it will appear long paragraphs of legal jargon varously captioned: Terms and Conditions of Sale, Conditions of Sale, Advice to Bidders, and so forth. If no catalog is issued, then similar material will usually be found tacked to a bulletin board or wall near the auctioneer's podium or in the area where the consignments are exhibited prior to sale.

Most prospective bidders ignore these notices, at least until they have a grievance, and auction gallery owners are well aware of that fact. Accordingly—and since it is in their own best interest that their customers know the "rules of the game" —it is customary for the auctioneer to hit at least the high points in his or her opening remarks to the audience, something like: "All sales are final here; payment by cash or certified check only. No goods removed till they are paid for."

You really can't expect much more from him. After all, if he reads the typical terms and conditions notice in its entirety, half his customers would leave or fall asleep before he finished. It does make tedious reading, but it is something you should be familiar with, because it directly affects every purchase you make and every complaint you may have.

Consequently, we have selected for analysis a typical example of such terms and conditions (though it is somewhat more lucid than most); and we will go through it paragraph by paragraph. The notice, that of C. B. Charles Galleries of Pontiac, Michigan, is as follows:

1. The sale of all items shall and will be conducted in accordance with the Uniform Commercial Code.

This paragraph, in effect, points out to the bidder that an auction is a sale like any other and that it is governed by those provisions of commercial law (contracts, fraud, warranties, and the like) which pertain to sales.

2. A bid by any person will be deemed to be conclusive proof that the person has made himself acquainted with these terms and conditions of sale and has agreed to be bound by them.

This is the old ignorance of the law is no excuse clause. If you are going to play the auction game you are bound to play by the rules. It becomes important, therefore, to know and understand the rules.

3. It shall be the duty of the Auctioneer to regulate the advance in the bidding and he may, at his discretion, reject a nominal or fractional advance, make final determination as to the successful bidder, and keep a sales record which shall be conclusive in all respects as to each sale.

Several important points are made in this paragraph. First, it is clear that the auctioneer must be in control of the bidding. Anything else would be chaotic. However, the auctioneer is interested in more than simply "regulating the bidding." He wants to have it proceed at a pace calculated to achieve a top price. If he can get bidders moving in $10 to $50 jumps, that will suit his purpose. Having some wise guy interpose a $2.50 bid will not. It interrupts the pattern of advance and casts doubt on the value of the merchandise. The conditions of sale published by Manhattan's William Doyle Galleries are more specific on this point, noting that the auctioneer may reject a bid if ". . . in his judgment said bid would be likely to affect the sale injuriously." Sotheby Parke Bernet goes even further, flatly stating: "The Galleries reserve the right to reject a bid from any bidder."

Secondly, the auctioneer has the right to ". . . make final determination as to the successful bidder." There will be instances where two bidders speak at once and each refuse to withdraw or to advance the bidding. In such a case, the auctioneer must resolve the dispute; or, as Doyle's provides, put the lot up for resale.

Finally, if questions arise as to who purchased a given lot or

Here is an Auction (with a capital A!) at its most dramatic and exciting. John Marion, of Sotheby Parke Bernet, auctions off "Icebergs," painted by Frederic Church in 1861. The price, $2.5 million, created a new world record for an American painting. Note the catalogs on laps and pencils in hand.

Courtesy Sotheby Parke Bernet

for how much it went, the auctioneer's written record will be considered the final authority. Not very democratic, perhaps, but a tidy way of resolving the matter.

4. Upon the fall of the Auctioneer's hammer and/or when the Auctioneer says sold, the item purchased remains at the purchaser's sole risk and responsibility.

What this means is that the bidder now owns the lot, subject of course, to paying for it; if it is damaged, his remedies are those of an owner. Until physically delivered to the purchaser, the auction house is responsible for the piece's safekeeping, just as a parking lot owner is responsible for your car. However, the gallery is liable for nothing more than the purchase price, even if the lot is worth far more than that on the market. Doyle's spells this out clearly, stating that ". . . If, for any reason, an article purchased cannot be delivered in as good condition as the same may have been at the time of its sale, or should any article purchased thereafter be stolen or misdelivered, or lost, the undersigned is not to be held liable in any greater amount than that paid by the purchaser."

At most large sales, the above would apply, since buyers do not customarily take immediate possession of their purchases. But, what about those country auctions where a handler deposits each lot in the lap of the successful bidder? There, you can have a real problem. For example, if you put your painting down by the side of your chair and a stranger sticks his foot through it, it's your problem. You still owe the gallery the purchase price, and your only remedy may be against your clumsy neighbor.

5. The highest bidder acknowledged by the Auctioneer is the purchaser and shall, after the sale of the item, give his name and address to the Auctioneer, pay the purchase price and remove said item from the premises. If purchase price is not paid or the item is not removed, the Auctioneer may, at his option, remove item to warehouse, cancel the sale and retain any payments made by the purchaser as liquidated damages, hold purchaser liable for the bid price, and/or resell the item for purchaser's account and risk, with purchaser liable for any deficiency, plus all costs of sale, warehousing and auctioneer's commissions.

The regulations regarding payment for purchases may vary from state to state and firm to firm. Large houses such as Sotheby Parke Bernet, Christie's and Doyle's customarily require full payment or a substantial deposit (usually 25 percent) prior to removal of the goods. Just how much they insist upon depends primarily upon your credit standing—in their eyes. Local and regional auctioneers, on the other hand, generally expect you to pay up and get the goods off the premises at the conclusion of the day's sale. Larger firms with more space give you two or three days to remove paid-for lots before they send them to storage. But even with the smallest rural auction houses, there are exceptions for dealers and others who have accounts with the firm or are volume purchasers.

> 6. The Auctioneer and/or Galleries has endeavored to catalogue and describe the items correctly, however, due to the nature of the items being sold, each item is sold in the condition it is in at the time it is sold.

This is the old "as is" clause designed to cover any errors made in cataloging items, as well as the possibility that a lot may be damaged or altered in some way (one of three bowls in a lot broken, for example) between exhibition and sale. Remember, if you are present at the sale, what you buy is what is actually put up for sale by the auctioneer, not what is described in the catalog—or even what you may see in the exhibition hall. Again, Doyle's puts it very succinctly: "The undersigned is not to be held responsible for the correctness of the description, genuineness or authenticity of any lot, and no sale will be set aside on account of any incorrectness, error of cataloging or any imperfection not noted. Every lot is sold 'as is' and without recourse."

Now, having said all these hard words, it is only fair to point out that auctioneers, themselves, do not always adhere to them. Not only will they take back (or "buy back" as they say) a counterfeit, but they will also sometimes accept a return when they feel there has been a genuine misunderstanding. With most firms, their reputation is worth far more than any one sale. On the other hand, they must protect themselves from tricksters like the one who will buy an item at auction thinking to resell it for an immediate profit and, finding this not to be possible, will attempt to return the lot on the ground of some minor or imagined defect.

> 7. Authority may have been given for bids to be made for and on behalf of the owner of the item to be sold, subject to a commission charge agreed upon.

Though somewhat convoluted in language, this paragraph simply tells us that some or all the lots may be subject to a

reserve (see chapter 7). Sotheby Parke Bernet states the matter
much more directly, noting that "Unless the sale is advertised
and announced as a sale without reserves, each lot is offered
subject to a reserve and the Galleries may implement such
reserves by bidding through its representatives on behalf of the
Consignor." Christie's follows the admirable practice of placing
a black dot beside each reserved lot number. As a general policy,
and whatever the type and size of auction house, you should
assume that there are reserves unless the sale or particular items
are listed as being unreserved.

> 8. The Auctioneer reserves the right to withdraw any item be-
> fore or during the sale.

The question of lot withdrawal has two facets. There is first
the situation where a piece is withdrawn after advertising and
exhibiting, but before the auction has actually begun. Such
withdrawal might be caused by damage, by problems with the
consignor, or by other factors. While it may be annoying to
you, particularly if you came some distance to bid on the withdrawn item, it seems clearly understandable.

More difficult is the question of withdrawal after bidding has
begun on the lot in question. The above C. B. Charles terms
would allow for this, and the regulations of most auction houses
are similarly worded. However, certain public relations problems arise if pieces are withdrawn after the bidding is well
underway (usually, of course, because the bids are not coming
up to expectations); so, usually a lot will not be withdrawn
after one or two bids have been made and accepted. Sotheby
Parke Bernet catalogs, for example, state that a piece may be
withdrawn ". . . if the auctioneer determines that any opening
bid is not commensurate with the value of the article offered."

> 9. Execution bids may be accepted by the Auctioneer as a cour-
> tesy to our client without charge, and the Auctioneer will en-
> deavor and undertake to the best of his ability, to execute such
> bids left with him as each item goes on the block, subject to the
> terms and conditions of sale herein and to such other terms and
> conditions as may be prescribed, and further subject to the con-
> dition that no responsibility or obligation shall result because of
> the omission, failure and/or refusal of the Auctioneer to execute
> any such bid.

This paragraph deals with the subject of left or absentee bids,
which is covered in chapter 6. It should be mentioned, though,
that the practice of absentee bidding, once confined to a few

If you were to bid on this lot at the Douglas Gallery in South Deerfield, Massachusetts, but hadn't attended the pre-sale exhibition or read the "terms and conditions," you'd be at the mercy of a "temple" where faith, hope ... and especially charity have no place!

large galleries, is growing rapidly as collectors and dealers try
to cover distant and conflicting auction dates.

> 10. It is our policy to protect the identity of any and all bidders
> at our sales, whether the bidder is present in person or has left
> an execution bid with the Auctioneer.

This provision appears in few other Terms and Conditions
of Sale, but the principle it sets forth is almost universally followed. For a variety of reasons, buyers wish to remain anonymous, and auction houses very properly respect that wish.

> 11. All sales are subject to sales tax where the sale is being con-
> ducted, and the sales tax must be paid in accordance with the
> law. Anyone buying for resale purposes must furnish and produce
> their resale tax number certificate should they wish exemption in
> payment of sales tax.

A provision such as this one appears in Terms and Conditions
published throughout the United States with the exception of
such states as New Hampshire, where no sales tax exists. Yet,
it is astonishing to see the number of buyers who express indig-
nation at having to pay a tax on "these old things." The law is
the law; and unless you are a *bona fide* dealer—and can prove
it via a state-issued sales tax receipt—the tax must be paid. In
the past it was usually sufficient to show your sales tax number
issued in your home state no matter where you were buying.
In the past few years, though, more and more states have begun
to insist that a dealer also have a tax number in the state where
the auction is taking place. Of course, there may be a fee for
issuance of such numbers, so the state position is quite understandable. For the dealer, it's just more expense and more paper-
work. And, no, the auctioneer won't overlook it; because in
many states if you don't pay the tax and he is audited, he will
have to pay it!

> 12. If within twenty-one days of the sale of any lot, the pur-
> chaser gives notice in writing to the Galleries that the lot so sold
> is a counterfeit, and if within fourteen days after such notice
> the purchaser returns the lot to the Galleries in the same condi-
> tion as when sold, and proves beyond reasonable doubt that the
> returned lot is in fact a counterfeit and that this was not indi-
> cated, the sale will be rescinded and the purchase price refunded.

An almost identical paragraph appears in Sotheby Parke
Bernet catalogs, and though some other major galleries do not
spell the thing out in print, it is highly unlikely that any responsible auctioneer would refuse to make a refund on some-

thing clearly counterfeit. You should realize, however, that the matter is subject to proof; your opinion, weighed against that of the house expert (who has something at stake since he may have "goofed") is seldom sufficient. It may be necessary to obtain an opinion from an independent authority.

13. If purchase has been paid for by check, other than a Certified Check, the Galleries reserves the right to withhold delivery until such check is cleared for payment.

In these days of "rubber checks," this paragraph requires little explanation. It should be noted, however, that galleries accept a wide variety of payment. While some still insist on cash or certified checks, others will take travelers' checks, personal checks, particularly if accompanied by a bank letter of credit, and even credit cards.

14. Bidding will be by number only. No bid will be accepted without the bidder having first obtained a bidding number from the cashier. To obtain a bidding number, a cash deposit of at least $100 is required. Additional deposits may be requested on special items at the time the item is sold at auction. However, a deposit greater than 25% of the bid will not be required. Deposit will be applied against purchase or will be refunded at the conclusion of sale at the bidder's request. It is bidder's responsibility to collect unused deposit.

Courtesy Chun Y. Lai

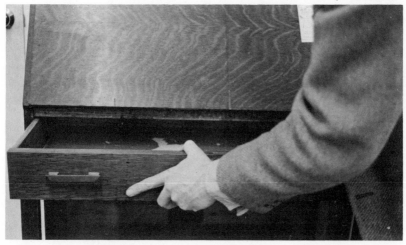

Here, a drawer is checked for any repairs or alterations.

The employment of a bidding number with cash deposit assures the auctioneer of a crowd of serious bidders. The system is, however, not commonly followed. The reference to additional deposits, of course, simply reflects the customary large gallery system of requiring cash deposits on sold lots.

A set of Terms and Conditions may also contain paragraphs other than those found in the C. B. Charles notice, though that one is unusually inclusive. For example, all houses employing the "10 and 10" system (see chapter 6) will have a statement advising bidders that they are obligated to pay a 10 percent premium on the bid price of their lot. Other information to be found includes notification, where appropriate, that the house is acting solely as agent for the consignors and owns none of the merchandise to be sold; that the legal rights of gallery and customer will be governed by the laws of the state in which the auction is being conducted, and that the order of sale will follow the numbered lots as they appear in the catalog.

And, of course, there may be other conditions dictated by the situation of the auction house, state and local laws or regulations, or the nature of a particular sale. In most cases, these will have little impact on you. Still, you'd be wise to protect yourself against unforeseen possibilities by taking a few minutes to read and understand the set of rules under which the auction is to be conducted.

5 How to Bid and Win

At auction, "Bidding is buying," as the saying goes. All the preparation that has led up to the sale, on the part of auction house and prospective buyers, has but a single moment in mind —that electrifying instant when the gavel falls and the word "Sold!" booms out over the audience.

The bidding process, itself, is far more complex than it might seem to the uninitiated. It involves a delicate tug-of-war between competing interests: those of the auctioneer and client, the consignor, and the prospective purchasers who oppose not only the auctioneer but each other. As more than one observer has noted, "There are no friends at auction."

To be a successful bidder, you must understand the bidding system in general and as it applies to the particular auction you're attending. You come prepared for the "contest" by having attended the exhibition, evaluated the pieces you wish to bid upon, and fixed a bidding limit (see chapter 3). Now, faced with a cajoling auctioneer and the temptation to bid against old rivals, you do not waver. When the offer reaches your maximum, you withdraw from the contest. Not one more bid, not two. You know what the lot is worth and when that figure is exceeded, you quit.

Nothing else to be said in this chapter is so important to the prospective bidder as this: You need great self-control to keep to bidding limits. If you have it (and, of course, the ability to evaluate the lots correctly in the first place!), you will rarely buy badly. If you lack it, getting "stung" can become a way of life.

The reasons for this are both obvious and less so. On the surface, the emotional, out-of-control bidder will be a prime target for the sharp auctioneer and for those nasty souls found at every sale who delight in running up opponents' bids, simply for the pleasure of hurting someone. On a more subtle level, however, if you know value and will bid only to a set point, you'll have little to fear from the "rings" (more about them later), your rivals or the auctioneer, no matter how unethical they may be. No matter what shenanigans may take place, if you stay within your limits, you will always buy well.

But, of course, you want to buy better than well. And that is where the question of bidding techniques comes in. First, there is the matter of how to bid. In many auction houses, potential bidders are furnished with cardboard paddles or sheets on which their bidding numbers are printed. If you wish to enter a bid, simply raise the paddle or card. And eventually if you are successful, the number on the bidding paddle is set down on the house records opposite the number of the lot sold or, lacking that, a description of the item involved. This system is the most efficient, but there are still sales where you bid by simply raising a hand.

You may, of course, also bid orally, usually by crying, "Bid!" "Here!" or the number representing the next appropriate increment, as "$25!" Most sophisticated bidders avoid oral bids on the theory that they both draw attention to the bidder (something to be avoided if you are, say, a well-known dealer whose lead in bidding is likely to be followed) and may project a sense of excitement or urgency that will stimulate opposition bidding. This hypothesis is doubtful, but it is true that oral bids assist rivals in locating you at a time you may prefer to remain *incognito*.

If you want to avoid having to bid by voice, you must be sure to sit where the auctioneer can see you (see chapter 3). Some houses with large halls and line-of-sight problems employ runners to spot bids and relay them to the podium. (These runners may also serve other, less beneficial, purposes as we shall see in chapter 9.) Wherever possible, though, bidding through spotters should be avoided. Confusion as to priority of bids and the figures involved may result when the offers are passed from bidder to auctioneer. In case of doubt, almost every auctioneer will take the bid he sees and close the bidding on it. At best, he may offer the person bidding through the runner another—but higher—bid.

Finally, some individuals use a number of subterfuges in an attempt to prevent their rivals from seeing them bid. They may hide behind poles or in corridors (see chapter 3). They may

Will this bidder "call it a halt" when he reaches his limit?

use hand signals or facial expressions which have been worked out with the representatives of the auction house prior to the sale. Otherwise, the removal of a hat or the tugging of a beard will be regarded as a personal idiosyncracy and not a commitment to buy. Contrary to popular belief, you don't have to sit on your hands and avoid all movement for fear of being mistaken for a bidder!

In fact, quite the contrary may be true, particularly in a large or crowded hall. When the bids come fast and furious, even the most experienced auctioneer may miss some. Moreover, in his spotting, inevitably he looks first to those who have bid previously. Consequently, it's a good idea to offer a few early low bids on lots you have no real interest in, just to let the man on the podium know where you are.

There are a few auctions (generally not in the antiques field) where, as soon as a lot is put up, everyone who desires to bid raises his or her hand or paddle. The bidding then advances by set increments, and the hands fall as bidders drop out, until only the buyer is left. Most auction-goers will never encounter this rather novel form of bidding.

The more usual bidding process is controlled by the auctioneer, who asks for an opening bid and then directs the advancement of the monetary increments. The exact procedure is a very personal, subjective matter, varying from auctioneer to auctioneer. It reflects, at least in part, the efforts of the bidders to distract the auctioneer from his path to the highest possible sale price.

The auction starts with the auctioneer calling for an opening bid or "opener" after describing the object to be sold and possibly noting that it was under reserve (a limit below which an item cannot go) or that absentee bids were made (see chapter 6). Since reserves and absentees operate as adversary bids for those in the house, because they may raise the price of the item, it is helpful to know they are involved. Unfortunately, though, some auctioneers let the bidders learn this for themselves.

In any case, the auctioneer will, typically, set an opening bid, saying, for example, "Let's have $5 for this vase." Then the auctioneer asks for increases or bids. While there is no set formula, the general rule is that he'll seek a bid about one-quarter to one-third of what he thinks the piece should realize. Sometimes a printed catalog with estimates is available. If so, you can compare these estimates with the requested openers

and get a pretty good idea of where the auctioneer is going—
or hopes he is going.

How serious the house is about a demand for a high opener
will depend on a variety of things, including the quality of the
piece offered, the personality of the auctioneer, and so forth.
In any case, the demand is likely to be tested by a counteroffer,
customarily a bid of one-half to two-thirds of what is sought.
This is a perfectly proper response, assuming it has some ra-
tional relationship to the value of the lot (you don't counter a
$100 demand on a $500 painting with an offer of $5!). Of
course, the auctioneer may reject your bid, even though you
consider it a fair one. The auction terms and conditions generally provide for the refusal of any bid (see chapter 4), and even
where they don't, auction custom recognizes the right of rejec-
tion of such counters, as well as withdrawal of the lot, if a more
generous offer is not forthcoming.

As a practical matter, though, reasonable counteroffers are not
generally refused. Auctioneers are in the business of selling
things, and they won't do it by antagonizing the audience. Besides, it isn't where they start that matters, it's where they stop!

The opening demand will not necessarily be a high one. Some
auctioneers like to encourage more general competition by
asking for a bid which is actually quite low in comparison to
the likely selling price of the lot. Ths is a two-edged sword. On
the one hand, it is likely to draw in bidders who might otherwise
not become involved, and it increases the likelihood of bidding
battles. On the other hand, too low an opener may cause some
prospective purchasers to assume that the example it not worth
much and to refuse to bid it up.

As a general rule, you are usually safe in bidding one-half
the demand on run-of-the-mill pieces, but you should be prepared to go higher on clearly quality merchandise—particularly
at the large galleries where few games are played and the auctioneer's demand is ordinarily realistic in light of market value.

Following acceptance of an opening bid, the auction proceeds.
There's no set policy as to what the next bid must be, but as
in the case of openers, the auctioneer has the right, whether it
is set out in the terms and conditions or not, to reject bids which
he regards as unreasonable and damaging to the sale. It is an
almost universal rule that a piece may be withdrawn if at least
two, and sometimes three, bids are not forthcoming. A rejected
bid is no bid, so usually you can forget about buying something
by adding a dollar to a $5 opener!

As a practical matter, you can learn what increments are acceptable to a particular auctioneer by watching him in action for a few minutes. If you're unable to restrain yourself for that length of time, usually you'll get by if you raise lots worth up to $20 by a dollar or two at a time; those valued at up to $100, $5 to $10 a throw, and those between $100 and $1,000, by $20 to $50, depending on how high the bidding starts. In these days of inflation, bids involving cents rather than round dollars are a definite sign of the amateur. Also, reducing your bid at the higher elevations generally is not tolerated, unless the house feels it has milked the lot for all it's worth and is ready to close out the sale.

The question of whether or not a lot will draw the two or three bids necesary to require its sale can be an important one, particularly at smaller sales. Since most merchandise at most major galleries is subject to reserves, which are usually exceeded in two or three bids, the situation is less likely to occur there.

There is nothing quite so frustrating as having your eye on a real treasure and seeing it withdrawn because you're the only one in the house bidding on it. Of course, this problem doesn't arise too often. Usually, a first bid will draw at least one follower. There are people who only bid when others do, and people who love to put in the second bid where three are required.

Naturally, you'd like to make the second and winning bid in such a situation—assuming the bidding stops there. One way to do this is to split up your auction party, so that your partner can make one bid and you make the other. In most cases, however, the house won't accept the two required bids from people who are sitting together or are obviously associated, so scatter yourselves throughout the room. Of course, this depends on how badly the auctioneer wants to unload the lot. If he is really out to dump it, he may even let you top your own bid in order to satisfy the two or three bid requirement. You never know until you try, and auction rules are made to be broken, particularly by the auctioneer!

Rules of the house aside, there is always the question of bidding tactics. Some people consistently pay less at auction and others pay more. To a great extent, good results reflect skill at beating the auctioneer and other bidders at the bidding game.

To be a successful bidder, it helps to be an amateur psychologist, adept at convincing other bidders that the piece you are making offers on is worthless, and auctioneers that you're too smart—or too cheap—to be trapped with false bids or other stratagems (see chapter 9). You may use a variety of ploys to obtain your ends; but of one thing be certain: that you are always aware of what's going on around you. Watch the auctioneer when you are bidding and make sure that he's aware of you. Keep track of your competitors, check the catalog to see if given lots are marked as reserved and watch out for shills and other tricks of the trade.

When you enter the bidding—and *exactly* when—will become a matter of crafty concern to you. You may, in some instances, want to give the opening bid. Particularly if things are going slowly, the auctioneer will appreciate your help in getting things started even if you quickly drop out of the competition. Somewhere along the way, the house may show its appreciation for your help by giving you a "fast knock" or giving a "deaf ear" to a competitor's bid.

What's a "fast knock"? The "knock" is a strategy used by auctioneers to attract attention and stir things up when the sale is going slowly. The auctioneer puts up a lot, asks an unusually low opener, and suddenly knocks the lot down to the first bidder without waiting for other offers. Since everyone thereafter hopes for a fast sale in their favor, they're likely to be more attentive and active bidders. From the point of view of the house, fast knocks are calculated sacrifices. If they can also be bestowed on steady customers or those who help to get the bidding started, so much the better.

You'll also come to understand or sense when a too-early entry into the bidding arena may draw in too many others, causing competition and a higher final price. It may also lead the auctioneer to believe that you are a "mark" who can be run up to a high figure. In order to avoid that, open a couple of lots and then quickly drop out, to let everyone know that you don't buy just anything.

You may also sit back and let the bidding progress on a piece you really want until you feel that it is reaching its limit. Then interject a bid. If everyone else is exhausted at this point, you may make off with the prize, particularly if you employ the sometimes devastating "jump bid." In this procedure, you enter a bidding sequence of, say, $10 increments and suddenly top the last bid by $30. Often the shock of this new and seemingly irrepressible foe in the field is enough to cause the opposition to collapse. Now, of course, you must understand that the new bid, shocking though it may be to those already in the field, is still below your self-imposed bidding limit. You would not make this move when at the top of your monetary ladder.

There are also dangers in entering the field late. If you wait a moment too long to slip in your bid, you may be behind the hammer. By and large, auctioneers would rather give up a lot to a bidder who has worked for it than to one who slips in at the last minute. The "working bidder" may be offended, and that's bad for business. So, if there is any doubt, the house may sacrifice the Johnny-come-lately extra few dollars and award the prize to the ostensible underbidder.

There is also the very real possibility that late bids may stimulate lagging bidding and draw in new rivals. After all, the reasoning goes, if this fellow is coming in so late, there must be something to be said for this lot. Weigh the pros and cons of the matter carefully, before you commit yourself. Don't bid on impulse.

Whether you come in early or late, jump bids or not, be consistent in only one thing—your inconsistency! By never allowing either the auctioneer or other bidders to be quite sure of what you are going to bid on a given lot, you'll discourage anyone from deliberately running you up. It will also make it difficult for others to know when—or even what—you will buy.

Before bidding, examine placement of the lots in the sale with care, particularly where there is no catalog estimate. Often this is your only clue as to what the house thinks things are—or should be—worth. This will influence how and when you bid— if at all. As a general rule, the better lots are found in the middle of the sale rather than at the beginning or end. Auction house employees, like anyone else, can make mistakes, so look for bargains which were incorrectly estimated or placed. And one of these days, you'll remain, waiting patiently late in the auction when many others have left, and when the auctioneer is thinking only of finishing off the consignments so he can go home. Having learned there are often good buys to be had in these "wee" hours, you'll be there to get them.

Of course, you won't be alone. Among your craftiest competitors are the groups of dealers or occasionally, collectors, organized in what are known in the trade as "rings." The theory of the ring is very simple. (In fact, nearly all auction attendees become "ringers" at one time or another.) A ring occurs when two or more prospective bidders agree among themselves not to compete for the same item or a group of items. For example, if two quilt lovers find themselves at the same auction, and two good quilts are being offered, it doesn't take too much intelligence for them to agree that only one will bid on each lot.

Such action doesn't, of course, assure them that they will get either quilt, since a third party can always outbid them; but, it does prevent the auctioneer from playing one of them against the other. And, most important, if there are no other "quilt people" present, it's likely that the collaborators will get the piece well below its true value. This, of course, is why auctioneers hate rings.

And, the organized, professional ring does function somewhat differently from our friendly, but quite amateurish collaborators. An efficient ring will consist of a major portion of those dealers in a given field (rugs are a popular area) who are present at a sale. It's not unusual for as many as a dozen participants to be included in the ring. Their goal, of course, is to stifle competition and to win desired lots at the lowest possible price.

Many prospective bidders are intimidated by a ring, a state of mind the ring members attempt to encourage. One of their tricks is to bid up collectors or uncooperative dealers on one or two lots, hoping to drop the merchandise on them at an unreasonable price, and scare them out of further bidding.

This tactic can work, but not if you follow your own rules and pay no more than your previously established limit for a lot, no matter who is bidding against you. Moreover, if you are a collector, you can always outbid the ring or any individual dealer, because neither can pay the retail price nor anything near it. They must buy cheaply enough to make a profit. If you understand this, you never need fear the ring.

Never underestimate them, either!

Another interesting tactic of the ring is the secondary auction the members hold to dispose of the items they've purchased. They meet at an appointed place and sometimes will even hire a professional auctioneer to sell off among themselves the newly acquired lots.

At the conclusion of the bidding in this "re-auction," the difference between what the ring paid for each item and what a member of the group bids for it is divided proportionally among the membership. Let's assume the auction price was $50, and the successful bidder in the re-auction offered $100. If there are five members to the ring, the winner takes the merchandise, reimbursing the ring for its $50 cost and paying each of the four members an additional $10. Thus, he actually pays $90 for the goods, and his cohorts each pocket $10 for not bidding against him.

In theory, it's possible under this system for a member of the ring never to take a lot, yet to make a substantial profit on each day's appearance. As a practical matter, though, anyone attempting this eventually will be excluded from the group and will be forced to bid against it. Generally, the members of the ring want the merchandise, rather than the few hundred dollars involved in the secondary sale.

There are several other fine points of bidding that you should be aware of. The first involves bidding on lots which consist of more than one item. Usually, a lot of this nature is sold as a unit, and this situation is set forth in the catalog or stated by the auctioneer at the time the items go on the block.

At times, however, several similar things will be sold together, for example, a grouping of five side chairs. The auctioneer will solicit bids for "the choice" or "the privilege." What this means is that he is asking for bids on a *single* chair, and the high bidder will have a choice of all the examples present. In most cases, you will have the right to take all the chairs at the bid price. If you choose not to take the whole consignment, the auctioneer will reoffer the other chairs. This is a perfectly proper way to sell, but it does occasionally cause confusion among inexperi-

"I hear a bid of $50 for this lot. Who'll give me $75?" Will you? (First make sure you're not bidding only on "the choice" or "the privilege.")

enced bidders, particularly if the auctioneer fails to spell out the terms clearly. It can be a shock if you think you just bought five chairs for a fabulously low $200, and learn that it will actually cost you $1,000 for the set!

When you are unclear as to precisely how a lot or a group of items is being offered, don't hesitate to ask. Misunderstandings of the sort described above are as embarrassing to the house as they are to the buyer. No auctioneer who creates awkward situations for his potential customers will remain in business long. In the same vein, be aware that any bid can be withdrawn or retracted at any time before the auctioneer brings down his gavel and hollers "Sold!" Everyone occasionally makes an unwise bid, either through sheer bad judgment or because they have somehow lost track of the bidding. A shout of "Withdrawn!" will cure it all. Now, of course, if you make a habit of this, it won't endear you either to the house or your fellow auction-goers. Fortunately, such occurrences are rare.

Another thing to keep in mind is that lots which are withdrawn because they did not reach the minimum reserve—or did not receive the required two or three bids—are not necessarily lost. Often, it is possible to buy them privately from the house at the conclusion of the sale. After all, the auctioneer knows that his audience will recognize the piece the next time he puts it up; he may be glad to take a fair offer, particularly if he isn't much of a gambler. Of course, this is more likely to occur where the gallery owns the lot than where he must deal with a disappointed consignor.

Finally, of course, we come back to you and your bidding technique. It can never be emphasized enough that you will be successful at auctions if you control your emotions, pay attention to what is going on around you, and treat the whole process as a business and not a game.

6 How to Bid When You're Not There

With the number of auctions increasing dramatically, it is becoming progressively more difficult to attend each sale at which you want to bid. Always responsive to their customers' needs, auction galleries have devised a variety of methods to deal with this situation. The two most common are direct communication between the absentee bidder and the auction room while the sale is actually in progress, and the use of "left bids" (also known as sealed, order or advance bids). In either case (with one exception which will be discussed later), the assumption is that the bidder is not present in the gallery at the time of auction.

Now, you might immediately ask, doesn't this system violate the fundamental requirement of good auction-going technique: that the bidder previously inspect the lots on which he is bidding? Not necessarily. In the first place, a prospective bidder may visit several galleries during the pre-sale viewings, to inspect the goods, make choices and then bid on them *in absentia*.

However, if you, as bidder, choose not to make an inspection, you'd rely upon catalog illustrations and descriptions and whatever you could learn through telephone calls to the gallery. Of course, descriptions never can replace visual inspection. On the other hand, you can find out a great deal by calling someone on the gallery staff and asking about the piece in which you are interested. Now, you have to take such information with several grains of salt, since the employee's job is to sell the lots. However, it's not unusual for bidders, especially volume bidders, to establish a close working relationship with representatives of auction firms. Heavy buyers at firms like Christie's and Phillips use the same agent over a long period of time and develop close confidential connections. The employee may receive a "tip" for his or her services, but this is generally frowned upon by the management.

During a major auction, the agents, sometimes collectively referred to as "the desk," sit near the auctioneer's podium, keeping in constant touch via open telephone lines, with one or more clients. They advise these customers of the state of the bidding and enter their bids, just as though they were present. In the past few years, the use of closed-circuit television (usually among various offices of the same national or international firm) has made it possible for the absentees actually to watch the proceedings. Consequently, a major piece may now be fought over by bidders from a dozen different states and a half dozen different countries.

However, the great majority of absentee bids are not handled in this manner. In most instances, the procedure requires you to fill out a form supplied by the gallery or to call in your bids so that the house may complete the form. Catalogs of most important sales include such a form for your convenience. It usually provides space for date, name, address and telephone number of the absentee, bank reference and signature, plus an area in which to enter the lot number, description and top bidding limit of any item on which a bid is to be placed.

Also, either on the form or elsewhere in the catalog (perhaps under Information for Intending Bidders) you'll find the house regulations pertaining to such bids. The provisions most often found in such regulations are as follows:

• Bids which are made by telephone or in person must be confirmed in writing or by telegram.

• The execution of absentee bids and notification of the bidders as to the results is a service offered free of charge. Successful bidders will be notified and receive an invoice setting forth the purchase, its total cost (including, of course, 10 percent buyer's premium where applicable as explained in chapter 4), and requests for shipping instructions. Unsuccessful bidders will not be notified in writing, though telephone inquiries will be answered.

• Since the service is offered as a courtesy, no auction house will take responsibility for failure to enter left bids or errors in executing them.

• In the event that identical bids are received on a given lot, that one which arrives first at the gallery will take precedence.

• Where payment is by personal check, unless the buyer is

known to the gallery, checks will be cleared prior to shipment of the merchandise involved.

Some firms also require that absentee bids be received a certain period of time prior to a sale (usually three days) or that bids be in even dollar amounts. And some insist on a deposit, say 25 percent of the total bids submitted. Deposits, naturally, are refunded within a few days following the sale, unless you have been successful, in which case they are applied to the purchase price.

In theory, of course, the absentee bid should be treated as a top limit, beyond which you won't go when you're bidding in house. Therefore, the auctioneer or the house employees (again, "the desk") should attempt to buy the piece for the absentee as cheaply as possible. In fact, most firm state this policy. C. B. Charles notes in its "Advice To Bidders" that "Lots will be bought as cheaply as is allowed by such other bids or bids executed in competition from the audience"; while Sotheby Parke Bernet advises that "Lots will always be bought as cheaply as is allowed by such other bids and reserves as are on our books or bids executed in competition from the audience." This is the proper way of dealing with left bids; unfortunately, there are some auctioneers who don't handle them in this manner.

The potential danger in the left bid is that the decision as to how to use it is largely left in the hands of the auction house. Ideally, the auctioneer will either announce at the start that there are absentee bids and that he and his staff will execute them, or (better yet) he will make this statement each time these bids exist on a given lot. This alerts everyone to the presence of outside competition and explains otherwise mysterious bidding procedures.

Moreover, properly used, order bids will be interspersed with bids from the floor in a normal sequence. For example, if the opening bid is $50, and the house has a left bid of $300, it would be correct to announce a "book bid" of $100. If floor bidders continue the advance, the left bid should then be employed in $50 increments (or, whatever other figure may be in operation) until it is exhausted or the opposition drops out.

What happens, unfortunately too often, is that the auctioneer uses the left or order bid to "up the ante." If the opening figure is $50 he weighs in with a bid of $150 from the order. If he gets away with this, he establishes a new increment and may realize more than he might have otherwise for the merchandise. If nobody bites, on the other hand, the book bidder gets the lot for

Courtesy Chun Y. Lai

Here is "the desk," famous (or infamous) as the administrative center where personnel record prices and numbers of lots as they are sold. Sometimes they also handle absentee (or phone) bids.

$150 where he or she might well have taken it for an even $100.

Another problem may arise with openings. It is perfectly proper for an auctioneer to use the order to open the bidding, particularly if the audience seems reluctant to get things started. Indeed, some firms prefer to do this in all cases on the theory that it may stimulate business to show that people not present are interested in the lot.

But, how much of the order should be squandered? That should relate in some way to the estimated value of the lot. You do not, for example, open at $50 on a piece estimated at $80 to $100. Yet, frequently auctioneers will throw in the entire left bid as an opener or "floor" under the bidding. What often results is that the first bid is the last, and the absentee pays far more than necessary.

To argue, as some do, that this is just—since the order bidder would have gone that high anyway—is no real answer. All of us have a limit at auction, but we are also entitled to purchase as cheaply as possible. You may be prepared to pay $300 (on absentee bid), but you'd prefer not to. You want the lot at the lowest knockdown price obtainable. By throwing in the whole bid early, the auctioneer prevents this.

The better auction houses (and quality has little to do with size) don't handle absentee bids in that way. But how do you know what's happening if you aren't there?

There are ways to tell, although usually they're after the fact. If you see that the house almost always makes your absentee purchases at the highest bid you authorized, be suspicious. Also, compare what you paid with the prices of comparable merchandise, on which you did not bid. If you seem to be paying more, probably you are.

Having made this discovery, you can solve the problem, not by ceasing to do business with the gallery (remember, they did nothing legally wrong), but by pointing out forcefully that you expect your bids to be handled with more consideration. Often, the auctioneer's awareness that you "know" is enough.

Opposite, Sotheby Parke Bernet, the world's largest auction house, in action. The podium is raised awesomely "on high." Above it hangs Sotheby's international currency converter.

Courtesy Sotheby Parke Bernet

Of course, you might also make it a point to pay a visit to a gallery where you have left bids. Actually, a lot of people bid absentee when they fully intend to appear in the audience to keep an eye on things. There are good reasons for such secrecy. Dealers, particularly major ones, don't care to let the competition know they are buying pieces or how much they are paying. This is particularly true today when periodicals in the field often report not only prices and descriptions of important items sold at auction but also, in some cases, to whom they were sold.

There are, in addition, the various personal rivalries and antagonisms which make it likely that a buyer appearing in person might be "bid up" by an enemy.

All problems aside, though, the absentee bid remains an important weapon in the auction-goer's arsenal—and one which may assume increasing importance as the fuel crunch and proliferation of auction houses make it harder for buyers to cover all the galleries where their money might be spent.

7 Paying Up, Packing Up and Returning "Lemons"

Like all good things, auctions must eventually come to an end. Sooner or later everything that will be sold is sold. You claim your purchases, pay up and depart. In most cases, there isn't much drama involved in this, but in many ways it is the most important part of the process and one which, like so much of the auction game, requires a bit of careful planning.

Payment is, of course, critical, and it should be handled properly. Though a lot of cash still changes hands in the auction galleries, there is no doubt that even this bastion of the greenback is gradually succumbing to the "plastic" and paper credit mania. Sure, there are a lot of sales advertised as "Cash or certified check only" or the cheerfully hopeful, "Cash or good check!" But you will usually find that, even here, a variety of payments are acceptable.

Whatever the mode of payment available at an auction, it should be determined before the auction begins. After you have made your "big killing" is no time to get into a discussion with the management over how you are going to pay for it.

Leaving the question of the type of currency until later, let's look at the matter of when, and in what manner, you will pay for auction purchases. Interestingly enough, this may vary greatly from sale to sale. Some of the largest galleries simply require that you register with the bookkeeper. You may or may not receive a bidding number or paddle (see chapter 6). When you've bought all you desire, you go to the "desk," make payment and either receive your lot or make arrangements for their delivery.

Other firms, such as C. B. Charles, require a cash deposit to bid (see chapter 6), and this deposit is then applied proportionally against all lots purchased. This procedure tends to discourage "bargain shoppers" who bid on a wide variety of items and then, when it's time to settle up, refuse to pay for or accept delivery of some which they decide they don't want. Since the deposit is spread over all the items bid on, the auctioneer can rightfully refuse such bargain shoppers delivery of anything, a situation usually not to their liking.

Even where deposits are not required as a requisite to bidding, some houses request them as lots are sold. In other words, when you are successful you're required to pay an immediate deposit (usually 10 to 30 percent of the sale price) on each object as you win it. Bid spotters or runners will go to the high bidder (they may or may not deliver your purchase to you at that time), take your deposit and issue a receipt. This system is generally unpopular as it interferes with bidding and requires the constant distraction of a small army of runners circulating through the hall.

Perhaps, the simplest system of all is the one still practiced at country auctions. As lots are sold, they are simply given to the high bidder or set aside for him or her. When you are through for the day, you go up to the bookkeeper, who has kept a record of purchases credited to your name, initials or number, and settle your account.

Whatever the procedure involved at a given auction, you should be familiar with it before the bidding starts. That avoids confusion and misunderstandings. Since this information is seldom set out in either the terms and conditions of sale or auction ads, it's a good idea to give the gallery a call a few days prior to the auction just to see what the rules are. If you are known to the gallery or have a good credit rating, it's sometimes possible to have the regulations bent to suit your particular needs. For example, many dealers who are regular clients of a specific firm run up an account, paying at the conclusion of the sale or, perhaps, on a weekly or monthly basis.

Checks are, with good reason, a source of concern to auctioneers. The number of bad checks issued at auctions has increased sharply in the past decade, so that galleries have tried to protect themselves in various ways. In some cases, only certified checks are accepted. In others, payment by check is allowed only when you have provided, prior to the sale, a letter from your bank attesting to your current solvency. You'll also find houses which accept checks, with proper identification, from banks within their state but not from those of other states.

Courtesy Chun Y. Lai

*Above is a typical regis-
tration desk, often loca-
ted near the front door.
Here you receive your lot
lists and bidding #s.*

Bank letters of credit are also generally acceptable, as are currency substitutes such as travelers' checks.

If you feel insulted by the limitations on payment by your check, don't! It's important to understand how little protection the seller really has against being cheated. Professional check kiters are a sophisticated lot. They seldom leave a discoverable identity; and even if they do, burdened local law enforcement agencies seldom pursue them unless the scheme involves many checks.

Over the past several years, the credit card has emerged as a viable solution to this problem. All the major galleries and many of the regional firms will now accept Master Card, American Express and other charge cards. While new government and bank restrictions on credit may affect this situation, charge cards are the answer to many problems of both auctioneer and buyer. From the point of view of the auctioneer, they are not easily counterfeited, and a reasonably efficient system keeps track of lost or stolen cards. For you, they are ideal for that big, unexpected purchase; they eliminate the need for hassling over checks or carrying large amounts of cash.

Whatever the procedures for payment, the written receipt is fundamental. You should not pay for anything at auction without obtaining a detailed receipt. First, get a receipt for any prepayments, such as the early deposits you gave in order to get a bidding number or to make a purchase later. In the case of a prepaid bidding number, the receipt simply reflects the deposit. In the case of an actual purchase, the receipt for deposit should contain the lot number and bid price of the lot to which the deposit is applied.

The receipts you obtain when you pay for your purchases should be even more detailed. They should contain not only the lot number and purchase price, but also a description of each and every item purchased. Where a lot contains more than one unit, each item should be separately described. Moreover, where a piece is specifically represented as being "of coin silver" or "by Rembrandt," this representation should appear on the receipt.

Don't imagine that all auctioneers will be delighted to provide such a document. Even the most honest of auctioneers will often wax eloquent about the origins of a piece of furniture ("Finest Chippendale chair I have ever sold!" for example), and then try to hand you a receipt for a "side chair," nothing more.

Questions of authenticity aside, preparing a detailed receipt takes time, often at a moment when other buyers are clamoring for a chance to pay up and get on the road. Still, the more detail you can get the better off you are, so stick to your guns! Why? It could prove very important if later you find you must *return* the piece in question.

Returns are not a favorite topic among gallery personnel, though all must deal with them at one time or another. By now, you know that items are sold "as is" and all sales are "final," caveats contained in all auction house terms and conditions. We have also noted the provisions of most better firms, covering returns where counterfeiting can be shown (see chapter 4). However, the fact of the matter is that nearly all auctioneers will take something back if they feel you have legitimate cause for complaint. It's a simple matter of business economics. A single sale is never worth enough to justify the bad publicity which could result from a nasty lawsuit or even just general "bad mouthings."

On the other hand, the law of *caveat emptor* (buyer beware) still applies in the auction mart. Unless you can show a deliberate oral or written misrepresentation of a material fact as to

Courtesy Chun Y. Lai

Beware the worn and damaged quilt. It's a poor investment.

origin or condition of the piece in question, you'll have difficulty prevailing in court. Appeals to local licensing agencies, better business bureaus and the like may actually prove more effective in the long run because they may threaten the auctioneer's entire business structure, whereas the civil suit usually deals with a single sale. On the other hand, "self help," such as loudly proclaiming the auctioneer's dishonesty or taking out an ad in the local paper to castigate him, is not recommended. Such things can lead to expensive libel or slander suits—more expensive than one bad buy.

The bottom line is that if you must make a return, deal directly with the auctioneer or other principal of the gallery, and be prepared to support your claim with documentary or expert evidence. Where a large sum is involved, and no cooperation is forthcoming, be prepared to consult an attorney. Fortunately, most disagreements of this nature never get to the litigation stage. The house refunds your money or it agrees to put the piece up for sale on your behalf. The sale-on-your-behalf situation, however, should generally be avoided since it is a real gamble. The piece may go for more; more likely, it will go for less. Too many people in the audience are going to remember it from last time around. Also, if the auctioneer insists on a re-sale, he should not charge a commission for his services, at least not unless the sale price exceeds what you paid.

A somewhat related problem is the purchase which is delivered damaged or not delivered at all. This really does happen. Things get dropped, stepped on or even stolen between podium and purchaser. As you now know, title to a lot is transferred to the purchaser on the fall of the hammer. This means that until he transfers the piece to you, the auctioneer is a custodian, known in the law as a bailee. If the piece is lost or damaged through his negligence, he is, of course, responsible, but only to the extent of the purchase value.

Since such occurrences are not uncommon, almost all auction houses carry insurance, and the usual procedure is to have you file a claim for compensation. It takes a few months, but eventually you recover. However, the auctioneer may offer to have the piece repaired or simply to refund the purchase price. Of course, what you really wanted was the object.

In a few cases, usually where the purchase was a "steal" bought well below market value, the claim of loss or damage is a subterfuge designed to cover up a house mistake in evaluation. If you sense that a cover-up might be in effect, insist on seeing the damage or "assisting" in the search for the missing item. Don't count on coming up with much, though. Anyone employing such a tactic probably will also get the piece into hiding as fast as possible.

The last, but hardly least, step in the auction process is packing and removing the purchases from the auction house premises. Every firm of any size has arrangements with one or more trucking companies which will, for a fee, deliver your purchases. Dealing with them is like dealing with your friendly local moving man. Get everything spelled out in writing, with specific commitments as to when items will be delivered, how they will be shipped, what it will cost, and so forth. Also make sure that the trucker's blanket insurance policy covers the full value of your purchases. If it doesn't, you can usually obtain further coverage for an additional fee.

Of course, most auction buys don't have to be shipped. You just load them in the car or pile them on the roof, and off you go. Remember that it's a good idea to bring boxes and packing materials to smaller sales and any sale where you might buy things which you can transport yourself. Cardboard boxes or plastic milk delivery boxes make the best carriers, and the air-filled plastic bubble pack is, by far, the safest wrapping material. Disposable diapers are also good, and old newspapers will do in a pinch.

If you don't have a van or station wagon, a rooftop carrier is a must. Movers' mats or old mattresses or blankets are also a must to cushion pieces of furniture, as are rope or strapping to secure them.

And, finally, check your personal property insurance policy to make sure that it covers things which you own while they are in transit. Many policies don't cover personal belongings outside the assured's home. If you're buying regularly at auction, you should have this coverage, even though it requires an additional premium. The greatest bargain is no bargain at all if it gets smashed up on the way home, and you have no insurance to cover the loss!

8 How to Make a Profit

Seemingly, the most obvious way to make money in the auction world is through buying well at sales and then selling the items at a much higher retail price. Buy low, sell high! Sounds familiar, doesn't it? Just like speculation on the stock market. But, we all know what can happen to stock speculators! The same is true in auction buying. There is just no certainty of your buying right consistently—particularly if your funds are limited. The highly competitive nature of the field, the influx of knowledgeable and moneyed collectors and dealers intent upon investing in art and antiques, and the efficient publication of auction sales that make "sleepers" less likely to occur—all these greatly reduce the possibility of "making a killing" on a regular basis.

However, that's not to say that you can't have fun and make a profit, too; you certainly can. It's still possible to make some fine buys at auction. Anyone who really likes the auction process is going to spend a lot of time on the scene, and if you do that you will learn what you need to know—about the auctioneer and how he does business; about what sells high in your locality and what doesn't; and about who the competition is. All of this, along with some sound knowledge of specific areas of antiques, should help you to turn a nice profit overall, if not every time out. And how many other businesses can you say that about today?

Unfortunately, for most people, "making a killing" is what the auction game is all about. People who are content with seven percent on their savings accounts, and who recognize that an appreciation of 20 percent in a year on a common stock is *not* common, enter the auction field fully expecting to double or triple their money on everything they buy. No doubt this does occur, particularly where prices, as in the jewelry and precious metals fields, may almost double in a few months. It happens often enough to *appear* to be the rule. This illusion is fostered by skillful auction gallery promotion which gets heavy press coverage for high prices and great buys.

But most killings or great buys are the result of fortuitous circumstances—buyer knowledge and auctioneer ignorance. For example, a few years ago a substantial eastern auction offered for sale a small lot of lead-glazed earthenware. Two of the pieces were clearly ordinary Mexican pottery, newly made. The auctioneer, glancing hurriedly at the pieces, assumed the others to be the same. It was late in the day, and he had long since cleared his profit. It was now, as they say in professional basketball, "garbage time," the time to sell out the last lots and get started on cleanup.

The auctioneer made some derogatory remark about "more of that Mexican junk" and knocked down the lot to the first bidder—for the grand sum of $1! What he didn't know was that the bidder was prepared to go to $400 for the lot—for, while two pieces were indeed inexpensive stuff from South of the Border, the third was a rare slipware plate from the Moravian settlements of North Carolina. The buyer knew this pottery and the auctioneer did not; but he was also lucky. In most auction audiences, there would have been at least one other person familiar with the ware and prepared to fight for it.

You can't count on being that lucky that often. On the other hand, if you are a knowledgeable and patient buyer, you can turn a clear profit over a period of time. To do so you must be aware of values and know where the market is going. This implies a more than casual familiarity with antiques, but it is a necessary familiarity—and a large number of successful auction buffs have it.

If you study auction results, visit good quality shops and shows, and seek out the companionship of knowledgeable collectors, in a relatively short time you'll get a good idea of the retail price range for the items that interest you. Determine the areas of the market which are moving forward—in price *and* popularity. Then confine your buying to your area of expertise and buy only the best you can afford.

The point about buying the best is hardly a revelation. Major authorities in the art and antiques fields say the same thing; yet it's often difficult to do this in practice.

An example: Let's assume that, as a knowledgeable collector and diligent observer, you concluded (correctly, by the way) that American quilts are one of the most popular areas of textile Americana. You studied the types and know the general price ranges. At auction, with a purchase fund of $500, you are faced with the choice of bidding on a single late-nineteenth century appliqué quilt with strong colors and in fine condition, or on several lesser and later pieces which, in toto, would cost as much as the finer example.

A quick calculation shows that the appliqué quilt should go for about $800, while the others (let's say there are three of them) would come to about the same figure—retail. Which do you buy? Over and over, the expert will say, "Buy the better piece," but most people will not. They will argue against putting all their eggs in a single basket (after all, suppose they can't sell that quilt?). They will insist that with three quilts they have a better chance of making a profit on one or all the pieces.

Experience, though, proves that the better piece will almost always prevail. Its price will go up higher and faster and stay there despite changes in the economic climate. Studies of auction prices during the great depression of the 1930s show that the better antiques lost very little value (there is always someone ready to buy a really good piece) while middle-range items dropped as much as 80 percent. Quality will out, and in every area, increased interest "pulls" lesser examples along, price-wise, as the best appreciates. Then, when interest wanes and the fad passes, it's the mediocre things which plummet. You'll do better now and in the future by choosing the best.

There are, of course, no real figures available on overall appreciation of items bought at auction. The general consensus among experienced dealers is that if you're a buyer who knows your field, and if you have retail or wholesale outlets for your merchandise, you can figure on making 25 to 40 percent profit on things you purchase at auction. It's not the great "killing" we dream about, but it's a profit margin that beats most businesses.

The magnificent example of Art Nouveau (opposite)—a spiderweb leaded glass, mosaic and bronze Tiffany lamp—established a new record when it was sold at Christie's for $360,000.

Courtesy Christie's

An auctioneer gets an
overview as house begins
to fill.

Courtesy Chun Y. Lai

Greater financial opportunities are available to you in the auction field. One handicap, however, is a lack of capital. If you don't have the money, you can't buy. There is a way to deal with this problem, though.

Auctioneers nowadays have money, in many cases a great deal of it. What they lack, however, is merchandise. With the increasingly competitive situation existing in the auction mart, it is difficult for gallery owners to come up with the high quality material necessary to mount an auction. No matter how successful and well known a house may be, it cannot know all the sources and have access to all the auctionable merchandise available. For this reason, every auction firm employs agents, people who scout out consignments and are compensated for it.

If you know a local auctioneer, it's possible that you can do this sort of work to your own benefit and profit, particularly if your job involves visiting people's homes. For instance, are you a local tax appraiser, a visiting nurse, or even a plumber? You see the interiors of many houses and eventually, you are going to see antiques. Some of the people owning these pieces will want to dispose of them, and you will be in a position to assist.

When you approach them, nearly all auction houses are delighted to cooperate in obtaining a consignment. There are two ways you can work together: You may draw up a letter of agreement between the firm and yourself in which you report your recommendation of the auctioneer to the consignor. This letter should also contain a paragraph setting forth your agreement on compensation for that service. It might read as follows:

Mr. Joe Smith
Smith's Auction House
Anywhere, U.S.A.

Dear Joe:

As I mentioned in my telephone call of August 8, 1980, I have recommended your services to: Mr. Henry Goodpackage, 343 East Pleasant Street, Anywhere, U.S.A.

Mr. Goodpackage is planning to put a collection of early Chinese bronzes up for auction, and I have suggested that you would be glad to handle them.

It is my understanding that if Mr. Goodpackage does place these pieces with you, you will reimburse me for my assistance by paying me one percent of the net price realized at auction for his merchandise. If this is in accord with our understanding, please initial and return to me the attached copy of this letter.

Sincerely,
Al Jones

If properly signed, this letter would constitute a contract in most states, obligating the auctioneer to pay you for your efforts.

Second, you might enter into an overall agreement covering any consignments you bring to the house. Fees for such assistance range from one to four percent of the auction proceeds for the goods involved. Sometimes you can make an agreement that'll give you a flat fee reflecting the value of the consignment. In most cases, the fee is not payable until after the sale has been held, though certain large firms pay all—or a portion—of the fee in advance.

There is another way to deal with the same problem. The auctioneer may "front" you the money to buy a consignment. That is, the house will cover the personal or business check which you use to purchase the goods. You then put the consignment through his firm for sale, and he takes out of the proceeds his commission plus the cost of the goods. You receive the remainder.

This sort of arrangement implies that the auctioneer has a great deal of trust in your ability to spot saleable merchandise. In effect, he's becoming your partner in the transaction and, in some cases, relying entirely on your judgment. The fact that such arrangements are common in the auction world indicates that this reliance is often well placed and mutually profitable.

9 Tricks of
the Trade

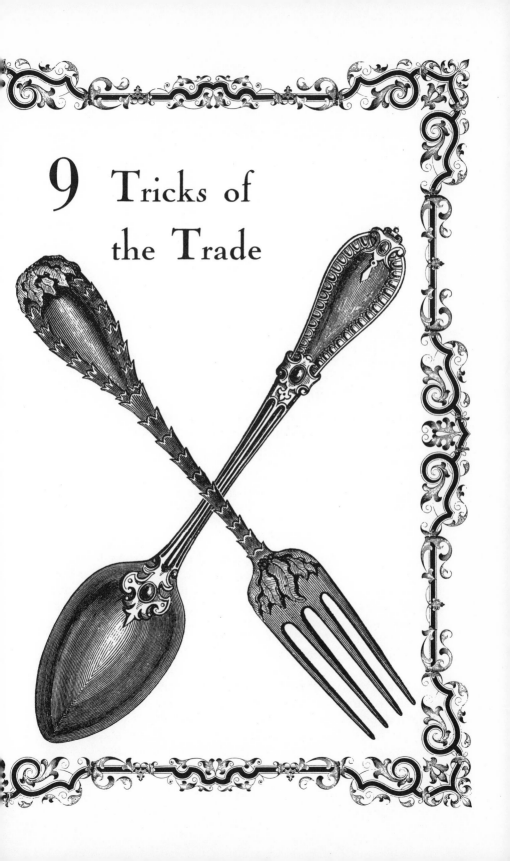

Complaints about auctions and auctioneers are traditional. Many of them have the venerability of age, having been raised off and on for generations.

Way back in 1828, in an open letter captioned, "Reasons Why The Present System of Auctions Ought To Be Abolished," an anonymous author argued that:

> Auctions produce, from their very nature, the Gross Fraud of Fictitious Biddings; an abuse which, it is believed, is almost universal. Who that knows anything of auctions can believe that all the sales made daily in this city are real sales? Who is there who does not believe that persons are sent by owners of goods . . . to raise the price on the ignorant and the unwary? Where is the buyer who is not convinced that many Auctioneers, while they are selling goods, make fictitious biddings themselves, to obtain higher prices for their employers?

Again, in the same year, an individual who signed himself "Plain, Practical Man" in his "Remarks On The Auction System," declared that, "It is a fact well-known that goods are frequently sold at auction bearing the conter-feit [sic] names and marks of manufacturers who excel in particular articles and so are imposed upon the unwary purchaser."

Reading these words, you may feel that little has changed over the years; yet, by and large, those abuses which do exist are limited to a small portion of practicing auctioneers and galleries. Most firms are honest and recognize that their continued success depends upon maintaining an untarnished reputation.

Nevertheless, there are sharp dealers in the trade, and no book on auctions would be complete without some discussion of them and their devices.

First, however, it's important to distinguish between illegal acts, fraudulent statements, and business practices which, while a bit sharp, are quite legal. Many buyers are outraged when a skillful auctioneer leads them into a bidding battle with another would-be buyer, urging them on with words like, "Come on, you have another bid in you!" or "You aren't going to let him whip you now, are you?" They get carried away and pay too much and blame the auctioneer. Likewise, there are those who, having been "too busy" to attend the exhibition, will bid frantically on what they think is a bargain, and then howl with rage upon discovering repairs, restorations and so forth. They forget that the seller has no obligation to point these things out, only to avoid outright misrepresentations.

Most of the instances of fraud and deceit relate either to the consignments or to how they are sold. As to the consignments themselves, you never can rely completely on the gallery's description of the merchandise, particularly as to its origin. It's common practice for auctioneers to sell their own merchandise (the presence of an antiques shop affiliated with an auction house is almost a guarantee of this) or items consigned to them by dealers. Since many buyers shun such overexposed material, the auctioneer may hide its presence among lots received from estates and other private sources. The phrase "and additions" included in an estate advertisement should be sufficient warning to the wise. A gallery which consistently advertises "estate sales" but never lists the names of any of the decedents, or "collections" while concealing the collectors' names, may be suspected of selling primarily dealer goods. Only a continual pattern of such action should be taken as proof of this, however.

A related scam is the fake "on premises" sale. In this case the auction house rents a large, old, vacant house in a rural area and then crams it full of dealer goods. Then it advertises the sale widely, usually with a prominent picture of the charming old structure, promising a houseful of "untouched eighteenth and early nineteenth century antiques." Usually, the only people who haven't seen these "lemons" are the people who lived in the house!

If you're suspicious of such a sale, arrive early and spend a few minutes talking to the neighbors. They may tell you the full story. If that doesn't work, look over the consignments. Do they really fit the house? Why is that rolled-up rug bigger than any of the rooms? Would a farm family *really* have owned six Oriental rugs and two Tiffany-type lamps? How come there is

Abraham Lincoln's beaver-skin top hat and the opera glasses he was wearing at the Ford Theater on April 14, 1865, when John Booth shot the President. These items brought $10,000 and $24,000 respectively at a recent Sotheby Parke Bernet auction, establishing a new record for a Lincoln relic. What's more, these high prices only confirmed what everyone knew: that historical memorabilia are hot!

Courtesy Sotheby Parke Bernet

sterling in the kitchen drawers and no china? Did they really cook only in eighteenth century wrought-iron pots?

Once you attend a legitimate house sale, you'll be able to spot the fake ones a mile away. There may be things to buy at such an auction, but the sort of person who'd create such a charade is also likely to be doing other nasty things.

Misrepresentation may be one of them. By now you know how important it is to listen to what the auctioneer says—but it is also important to disregard a good portion of it! No one, for example, should buy a chair for a high price simply because the seller represents it as "Chippendale." It's confusing to identify authentic period pieces—made during the time a certain style was in vogue—and furnishings made in the same style at a later date. For instance, there are signed Tiffany lamps, Tiffany-style lamps—and then there are new Tiffany-style lamps! Better galleries carefully distinguish "period" from "in the style of" furniture—but beware the irresponsible auctioneer who may try to pass the latter for the former!

Some of the Queen Anne- and Chippendale-style furniture made in the late nineteenth and early twentieth centuries is very well done, and inexperienced collectors can be fooled. If your auctioneer maintains while he is selling it that a piece is "Chippendale," he should be willing to put that on your receipt. If he isn't willing, demand that he take the piece back. Otherwise, you may be taking a big chance in making the purchase. The price is often a good clue. There are few auction houses today, even in the remotest areas, where good period furniture doesn't bring big money. If you seem to be getting a steal, you are probably getting robbed.

Paintings are another area where misrepresentation is rampant. You'll find altered pieces, such as those where a signature or some other symbol has been added to an unsigned work to enhance its value; a perfectly decent painting of a European sailing ship may "acquire" an American flag in order to make it more appealing to local collectors, for example. If you know your paintings and have your black light handy at the exhibition (see chapter 4) you can spot these problems.

Then there are many signed and unsigned paintings which are attributed to recognized, and sometimes important, artists on the basis of style, color, subject matter and so on. The major galleries carefully distinguish paintings which they warrant as being by a specific artist from those which they feel *may* be by him or which are by individuals in some way connected to him.

Christie's, for example, lists the artist's name only where they represent the work as painted by him. The phrase "attributed to" preceding his name means only that it *may* be his work, while "in the manner of" denotes a work, usually of a later period, done in the artist's style. Other phrases, such as: "circle of," "school of" and "studio of" reflect still different relationships to the artist.

Some auctioneers will freely offer an etching as a Rembrandt, or a Miro, without attempting to make any such distinctions. Again, if he says it, he should be willing to put it in writing. And if the auctioneer does say an oil is "school of Winslow Homer," for example—and you buy it as a Homer because you haven't read the terms and conditions of sale (and don't understand the difference)—you'll find that you have little recourse. The best defense against misrepresentation and improperly attributed merchandise is personal knowledge and a careful examination of the lots while they're on view.

The subterfuges used in selling are another thing entirely. They, too, often depend for their success on a buyer's lack of understanding and attention. Auctioneers, honest or otherwise, thrive on emotional, aggressive bidders. They love to have you tell them where you'll put that couch after you win it. They are also pleased when you take the time to tell them you noticed the bad crack in the porcelain vase or the replacement finial on the highboy. Both statements tell them that you're a hot prospect—someone who really wants the lot in question and can probably be induced to bid more than it's worth.

Slightly unscrupulous auctioneers will try to get you to give them that high bid in several ways. They may use the services of one or more shillabers, or shills, as they're commonly called. The shill is an auction house employee who sits in the audience and bids against legitimate bidders. His or her goal is to keep the action going until the bid reaches a certain minimum figure whch has been previously set by the auctioneer. With such a character in on the action, you won't "steal" anything, at least not anything the house recognizes as valuable.

Shills may or may not be recognized by others in the audience, depending on their skill and the frequency with which they're employed. Some are extremely obvious, but even when they're not, certain characteristics always define the shill. He or she may buy heavily, but with no discernible pattern. For example, the shill may buy a lot of silver, then a piece of furniture, then a box of Depression glass and a rug. Since most dealers and collectors confine their activities to one or to just a few areas, this activity is cause for suspicion.

If such characters emerge at an auction, watch to see if they make note of their purchases, lot number, costs and the like. Most buyers do this, and it is especially unusual for heavy buyers to fail to keep track of their acquisitions. How do they deal with small, fragile and valuable lots? Shills, typically, don't like to handle such things for fear of loss or breakage. So they're likely to tell the auctioneer to "hold them"—exactly the opposite of the honest purchaser, who would want to wrap them up and pack them away for safekeeping, since he owns them now.

Also, it pays to see what the auctioneer is doing with the supposed shill's purchases if they are not delivered to his seat. Are they put aside with the rest of the lots being held for different bidders, or are they segregated? That would make it much easier for the house to put them back in storage for the next sale.

Another clue as to who is doing the house's work is the way the shills bid. Characteristically, they come in after a legitimate offer has been made. In fact, an auctioneer who is a real gambler will instruct his shills (if he is using more than one) to bid one after another, thereby boosting the price two jumps. This sort of "pyramiding" can only be used sparingly except with the least sophisticated audiences, so probably it will only be tried once or twice during the sale.

Also, only the very best shills are accomplished actors. Since most are not, they can seldom mimic the real tension under which most bidders operate. Even at the highest figures, they're likely to snap out a quick figure where real bidders would hesitate or allow anxiety to show in their faces or voices. And as the evening wears on, the shill is apt to perform with a singular lack of enthusiasm.

Now, of course, the shill's role is to buy nothing! It's to make you pay more for what you buy. Every "purchase" he makes marks a failure for the house—another lot that will have to be offered again in the future. On the other hand, the shill and the auctioneer are engaged in a frantic guessing game. How high will the bidder go? How far can he be pushed before he drops out? Some shills are better at this guesswork than others or, perhaps, less greedy. In either case, they get help from the auctioneer. Sometimes a duped buyer passes when the bid gets too high, only to have the shill suddenly exclaim: "That wasn't my bid!" or "Whose bid?" or some other indication of confusion.

*In a small house the
"block" is up against
back door!*

Courtesy Chun Y. Lai

Whereupon the relieved auctioneer responds, "Okay, I'll let it go this time, but watch what you're doing. Sold to the underbidder!" Needless to say, this hustle is good only for one shot per shill a night.

So what do you do if, after all this, you're convinced that you have spotted a shill? Do you run down front and accuse him and the auctioneer? Do you punch him in the nose? Hardly. This sort of connivance is a form of fraud—a form extremely hard to prove. Accusing someone of it in front of an audience could lead to an unpleasant lawsuit. Sure, you could file a complaint with the local district attorney; maybe, he would send someone around to investigate. Probably the best way to show your annoyance would be for you and your party to walk out after some particularly obvious buy-in. With many knowledgeable people in every auction crowd, this sort of walkout could get infectious. When the rest of the audience sees people leaving, they, too, will become suspicious, even if they don't quite know what's going on. It can work; I've seen it happen! And, once you leave, stay out. Don't attend that auctioneer's sales in the future. In most areas, there are enough auctions so that you can give up one. And a boycott can be damaging enough to a gallery to force a shift in policy.

For the auctioneer who can't afford to employ a shill—or who prefers to have everything under his own control—there are other ways of running up the bids. "Phantom" bidders, for example. At first blush, it might seem inconceivable that an auctioneer would have the nerve to stand up in front of hundreds of people and just make up bids. But it's done all the time.

It usually happens when a single bidder is battling for a treasure against what seems to be an unusually stubborn opponent. The auctioneer will, perhaps, point to the real bidder as he or she makes an offer, then look back toward the rear of the building or into a dark corner (always some place the bidder can't see well) and "acknowledge" an opposing offer. There will be no one there, of course!

If he is dramatic (many country auctioneers seem to be frustrated actors), the auctioneer may even seem to cajole and urge on his "phantom" bidder. He may ask him if he wishes to go higher (seemingly straining to get an answer), or encourage him to "give it another try." What he doesn't do, though, is send the lot down so this phantom can examine it more closely! When auctioneers who usually pass around the lots to stimulate bidding suddenly stop that tactic, it is frequently an indication that someone is being "run."

The really sharp auctioneer will use his phantom sparingly, interjecting a bid here and there among legitimate offers. He raises the ante gradually, so as not to scare off the real bidders. For, remember, if he misjudges, and the "pigeons" quit, the house loses a sale.

It is the very nature of the bidding system that allows the "phantom" ploy to work. After all, in almost every audience there are a few secretive bidders hiding in corners or making their offers through signs and gestures. Since the crowd can't see them, it's reasonable that they can't see this "bidder" either.

How can you tell if you're up against a "phantom"? It is easiest at an auction where lots are taken immediately to their winners on the fall of the hammer. Phantom "bidders" can't accept their merchandise, of course, since they aren't there! Now, other bidders also may not want to take their lots at the moment, but usually you can see them indicating that. If there are bidders who consistently request that their pieces be left at the podium and whom you can't ever seem to locate when— or after—they are bidding, you probably have phantoms.

Again, what to do? Some auction-wise people will suddenly sing out, "Where was that bid?" or "Whose bid?" The shock effect of a public query can be substantial, especially since others are sure to be wondering about all those silent bids, too. It takes a bold and experienced faker to face down such a question, particularly if it is raised several times by different individuals. Indeed, if you believe an auctioneer is using this stunt, it may pay to attend his next sale with several other people. Then sit in different areas and independently question the bids.

Another effective device is to move to the back of the hall or some other vantage point. Stand there quietly but visibly eyeing the bidders. Nothing need be said; indeed, as in the case of the shill, it's best than nothing be said. Shouted accusations seldom achieve anything other than getting you branded as a "nut" or a "sorehead" who's angry because you lost a lot or paid too much. Be a crusading auction-goer and be forewarned that your efforts may not be appreciated. Believe it or not, some people love to be fooled. And some, once fooled, want others to be, also. Still others may know what is going on but resent your butting in, particularly if you're an outsider. Discretion in these matters is always advised, particularly in strange communities.

Sometimes, you are told the phantom isn't in the auction hall.

The auctioneer will announce before bidding begins on a particular lot that he has an absentee or order bid on it. Such bids (see chapter 6) are, of course, perfectly proper. The problem is that it's practically impossible to tell whether or not there really is such a bid on the lot. If there is, well and good. If there is not, you are just being "run" again.

The usual way in which the unscrupulous auctioneer will use the fake order bid is to interject it between one or more live bidders to force them up, without ever revealing just how far the "absentee" will go. There will come a point, depending upon house greed or judgment, when the piece will be knocked down to someone in the audience.

The phantom order bids may be made by the auctioneer himself or by a third party, such as a clerk or the cashier, who will call them out. This requires coordination; the employee needs to know how and when to stop. Done well, the third party method often seems more authentic.

If the auctioneer isn't too sharp, you may be able to spot the phony absentee bids through the way he handles them. If, for example, he usually refers to a separate sheet when handling legitimate order bids, his failure to do that may indicate that he is playing games. Likewise, if lots won by "real" absentees are segregated in some way (stacked to one side or behind the stage) and certain other alleged absentee merchandise isn't

All eyes seem to be asking, "Is there a phantom bidder here?"

handled the same way, that may indicate it has really been bid on by the house.

Of course, the auctioneer has the same problem here that he does with the shill and the phantom bidder. If he pushes the real bidders too far and they drop out, he must buy back his goods and wait for another day.

Finally, the auctioneer may use the nonexistent "reserve" as a way to boost the price. Reserves are becoming so common today that they no longer (as they once did) arouse immediate suspicion in the audience. Consequently, they are growing in popularity among dishonest auctioneers. One problem with the reserve, though, is that—legitimate or not—it intimidates some potential buyers. The mere fact that a reserve is announced, or that there is a feeling in the crowd that reserves are in effect, has a chilling effect on the bidding. This is especially true where the bidding is opened with a reserve bid (see chapter 5).

Accordingly, most auctioneers who use fake reserves prefer not to start the bidding off with them, but rather to interject them as the bidding progresses. What they may do is have a shill open the action, and then throw in the reserve. It is theoretically possible to have a string of a half dozen bids, only one or two of which are from real bidders!

Bidding on the reserve is handled in much the same way that absentee offers are. And the same clues as to its bogus nature may be present: unusual segregation of the lots, reference to a separate listing, and so forth. But, again, it's difficult to spot this form of chicanery if it is handled with any competence at all. On the other hand, the more these ploys are used, the more likely it is that potential victims will drop out too soon. That means more consignments that must come up again in the future, and many auction-goers remember that sort of thing. If you keep seeing the same merchandise over and over after it was ostensibly "sold" weeks ago, you begin to get the picture. So, in all cases, the best "runners" are those who use their tricks sparingly and know when to stop.

From your point of view, on the other hand, all the cleverness in the world in spotting bad actors is not half so valuable as the self-control necessary to stop within your bidding limit. If you can master yourself, you won't get hurt. You may or may not get bargains at rigged auctions. At some you won't be able to buy at all. But you will always be protected if you can achieve that discipline.

10 How to Become a Successful Seller

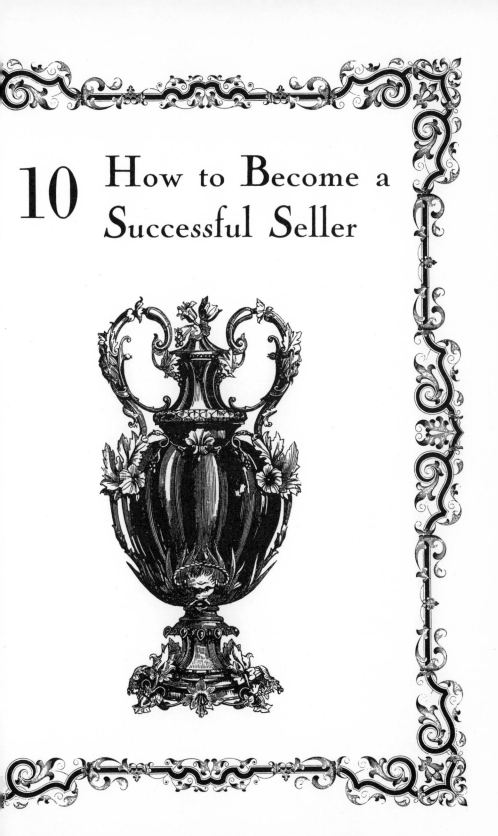

Pick up a periodical today in the antiques and art fields or, indeed, just the local newspaper, and you'll be overwhelmed by the most recent auction news: the painting that sold for a half-million after lying unrecognized for a century; the tiny bronze that brought $40,000; the quilt that sold for $7,500—on and on it goes. It's as though all the attics in the world are being emptied and their contents turned to gold on the auction block.

Is it really that easy? Are all prices that high? Well, to answer both questions: no and not always. For many objects and under many circumstances, a sale at auction is the best way to obtain the top price. However, to make the right decision and to get the best deal, you need some knowledge of the pro-and-cons.

Buying at auction, as you know, is generally a gamble. Selling is, too. But as seller, you're in a position to balance the odds in your favor. For one thing, the key actor in the auction drama, the auctioneer, is on your side. Since the house commission is based on the sale price, it is absolutely in the auctioneer's interest to get the highest price possible. This, of course, is also true in cases where the gallery owns the merchandise it is selling, but in this chapter we are dealing only with consignments.

For another thing, you have a "fail-safe" device with which to protect yourself (at least in part) from unexpected and unprofitable results: You can place a reserve on your merchandise. A reserve is, as you know, a price below which the piece will be withdrawn by the house—"bought back,"— as the saying goes. In most cases the bidder will never even know this has happened, since the auctioneer will make it appear that the piece has been sold to an absentee bidder.

Interestingly enough, when the word "reserve" comes up, you'll often find that the close relationship between consignor and auctioneer becomes "cooler." Auctioneers, as a group, don't like reserves, though they recognize the need for them. After all, the auction gallery is in the business of selling, and if the auctioneer doesn't sell, he doesn't get paid. It's very frustrating to him to invest time and money in promoting an object, and then see it fall short of the reserve and fail to sell. Reoffering the piece at a later sale is not a solution (though many firms do it out of necessity). Auction-goers frequently figure out what has happened when a supposedly "sold" piece suddenly reappears on the block, and it becomes even harder to get a good price the second or third time around. The merchandise becomes an albatross which must eventually be sold below reserve or transferred to a distant firm with a different clientele where its history isn't known.

The galleries show their distaste for reserves in two ways. First, almost all auction houses assess a penalty (usually up to five percent of the low estimate) against the consignor on bought-back goods. Since the owner must also pay insurance, shipping and other incidental costs, whether or not the object is sold, the owner's loss can be substantial. That penalty, however, rarely covers the gallery's loss on the deal. In short, a buyback is a loss all the way around. Reserves should always be realistic, and based on a professional analysis of the market rather than wishful thinking.

Some auction galleries feel so strongly about this problem that they simply refuse to accept reserved merchandise, but they are in the minority. Most auctioneers allow reserves on certain pieces, usually the more valuable ones. And with the growing public consciousness of values, it's increasingly difficult for galleries to obtain quality material without honoring reserves.

Clearly, the reserve system—and the auctioneer's role as ally —are major factors in encouraging people to dispose of their heirlooms through auction. But there are other ways to sell, and in some cases, they work out better.

The private, direct sale, for instance, requires that you, the owner of the goods, have some knowledge of the antiques and art markets, that you know their approximate worth, and where and to whom you can sell them. Highly specialized collectors often sell very well privately, since they know their field (through buying in it for years), and usually many of their fellow collectors (the potential market), as well. The antique toy or beer stein collector, for example, may know individuals who have been coveting some of his pieces for years. Such buyers may even pay a premium to keep a piece from going to auction where they might pay more or even lose the treasure to a competing bidder.

Unfortunately, though, most owners neither know their possession's value nor where to sell it. In this case, it's highly unlikely that they can realize more than a fraction of what they could obtain at auction. Even astute collectors may have problems, particularly if they wish to sell varied collections. They'll find that their fellow collectors don't want everything, but just to "skim" the collection, buying the top pieces—which add value to the group as a whole—and leaving the rest to the seller.

Faced with these problems, both knowledgeable and not so knowledgeable owners may resort to selling wholesale to a dealer. The dealer is more apt to make an immediate decision, buy everything, and pay cash. But problems arise here, as well. The dealer rarely can afford to pay more than one-half or two-thirds of market value. He has overhead to think of, a profit to make on resale and, in the back of his mind, the gnawing thought that perhaps the items won't sell—or at least not for what he hopes.

So, sooner or later, the owner starts thinking about auctions again. Now the question is: What firm or individual will do the best job? Part of the answer to this dilemma has to do with the nature of the merchandise: Certain things sell far better in cities than in rural areas, in one section of the country rather than another. Bronzes, for example, bring high prices in New York City and Los Angeles galleries, but often only a pittance in midwestern or rural New England auctions. On the other hand, until recently, Pennsylvania and Massachusetts dealers were buying American country furniture at Manhattan auctions at prices so low that they could auction them off again in their own area!

Now, of course, most owners don't know about all that, and tend to turn to a local auction house. How do you choose the right one? In most areas, there are several choices, but unless you know an auctioneer personally, there's no better guide than reputation. Is the candidate a member of the National Associa-

The rare and special American quilt, opposite, is a pieced, appliquéd and trapunto floral that sold at a record $6,500. Quilts are "hot" now.

Courtesy Sotheby Parke Bernet

tion of Auctioneers or a state or regional group? That would indicate interest in his profession and living up to certain standards. How does he run an auction? Go to one and find out. It isn't difficult to find people who have something good or bad to say about the man on the podium. There are other sources of information, as well. Who does your banker use for estate auctions? Who does your lawyer recommend? If you have friends or associates who have put goods through a local auction, what did they think of the results? Sooner or later by asking questions and going to auctions, you'll choose an auctioneer who will answer the big questions of how and where to sell your goods.

Should the items be sold as part of a general or miscellaneous auction, or held for a sale specifically related to their field? Certain firms specialize in a limited area. For example, the Theriaults of Waverly, Pennsylvania, handle dolls, while Barridoff Gallery of Portland, Maine, sells only paintings and sculpture. Nearly all larger galleries and many smaller ones hold some specialized auctions each year; the subject matter may range all the way from Oriental rugs and continental porcelain to tin toys or duck decoys.

If you have several pieces of a type and quality suited to such a specialized sale, that is often the way to get top prices. Properly run, specialized sales will bring out the top dealers and collectors in the field, because the auctioneers who run this kind of sale know how to reach them, and how to get maximum effect from their advertising. Unlike the general auction, which serves as a form of entertainment for at least some of the audience, the specialized auction is usually packed with fanatics eager to buy. Few of them sit on their hands!

But there are certain very real disadvantages to specialty auctions. They are few and far between in most areas of the country. In order to have your pieces included you may need to ship them far across the country and wait six months or more before the sale takes place. Moreover, the specialists' standards are high, and you may discover that they have no interest in the items which your local auctioneer would gratefully accept and work hard to sell.

The question of the general vs. the specialized auction house relates to the one of the local vs. the national auctioneer. For most merchandise, the local or regional house is usually the better bet. It is nearby, which means that your goods don't have to be shipped to the far corners of the earth many months before a sale. Also, since most locals hold an auction each week, or every two weeks, the goods are sold more quickly and, almost invariably, you get paid in a much shorter period of time. The larger auction houses, which hold the specialized auctions, have made real efforts in recent years to speed up payments to consignors, but distance and sheer volume make it almost inevitable that it will take a month or more following the sale to get your money, and in some cases as long as six months.

Another advantage in dealing with locals—and one which few people know—is that locals often are willing to advance you money against the sale of your goods. This does not mean that the gallery buys the merchandise. An experienced auctioneer can, by just looking at a potential consignment, get a pretty good idea of what it will bring on the block. So if you need cash he will frequently advance you a portion of that figure as a courtesy, say 10 to 30 percent. National auction houses will rarely do this.

All these benefits aside, there are certain times when you must sell on a national level, even though it means delay in sale and payment and a certain loss of control. For the best merchandise, say a Tiffany floor lamp or an eighteenth century highboy, there is no beating a catalog sale at a famous New York, Washington, London or other major European gallery. (Certain items actually will bring enough in Europe to justify shipping them there for dispersal.) The difficulty may lie in convincing your local auctioneer that the goods should go out of town if you have first approached him. After all, he wants to sell them—for profit and prestige. If he arranges for their sale through another gallery, he receives a forwarding fee, but it doesn't begin to compare with his commission on a direct sale.

Often, the solution is for you to contact one or more major galleries directly. These houses advertise regularly in publications such as *The Magazine Antiques, Hobbies* and *Antiques Monthly*, as well as in travel and arts periodicals and newspapers in larger cities. Such firms as Sotheby Parke Bernet, Christie's, Morton's in New Orleans and Sloan's in Washington, D.C., to name a few, usually are willing to send representatives to look at quality merchandise. The best way to approach these galleries is by mail. It's difficult to convey much in a telephone call, but a letter containing accurate descriptions and good quality photographs or 35 mm slides will often elicit an immediate response. Accuracy is very important here. You may not know what you have, but if it is well photographed and described, an expert will.

It's a good idea to "shop around." Auctioneers realize that any reasonably astute consignor will look for the most advantageous deal and try to get the best terms as to commission, advertising, time of sale and payment. Any good firm puts its cards on the table and lets you make up your own mind. In choosing a gallery, your major concern is to obtain the services of the firm you need, on the most favorable terms.

The auctioneer's concerns are different. At the moment, because of the great boom in auction buying, nearly every competently managed gallery is earning a profit. Money, they have; what they need to keep going, as you know, is merchandise. If you remember this, you'll be able to negotiate the terms of your consignment from a position of strength. How strong your position is will depend on the quality of your merchandise. If you own desirable items, you'll do well; if you are trying to consign junk, don't expect any favors.

The two basic negotiating areas have to do with money and terms of sale. In the money category is the auctioneer's commission (a matter of prime concern to both parties). The commission is that percentage of the gross sales price that the house keeps as payment for its services.

The nature of the commission has changed greatly in the past few years. Not so long ago, it was rather firmly fixed by most houses at 20 to 30 percent. However, the introduction of the "10–10 system" has greatly altered things. The rationale behind charging buyer and consignor 10 percent each was that a lower commission would encourage consignors to give up their goods, rather than hold onto them or sell them privately. The idea behind this system (borne out in England where it was established) was that buyers would grumble, but would keep right on buying. That judgment has proven sound. Bidders just add on the 10 percent surcharge in their bidding calculations, and the auction frenzy continues. The auctioneer still gets his 20 percent—10 percent from consignor and 10 percent from buyer —and also an increased flow of merchandise.

Twenty percent is not an unreasonable commission considering that auction costs generally run to about 14 percent (broken down into 1 percent insurance, 1 percent catalogs, 2 percent advertising and 10 percent general overhead. True, some of these costs may be partially offset by such things as consignor payments and catalog sales, but the bottom line is not that fat. To succeed, the auctioneer must deal in volume.

So, you can anticipate that the auctioneer will ask about 20 percent (10 percent if he is operating 10–10) for his services. However, this figure is always open to negotiation. Galleries using the 10–10 system have been known to take merchandise

It is here, at the cashier's table, that you settle up, paying for the lots you've won and arranging for their disposition.

at no commission whatsoever when they felt that it was prestigious to have the material in the house, and when they expected that the 10 percent buyers' commission would be high
enough to make for a substantial profit.

Just how far below the standard commission you can get the
auctioneer to go depends on the quantity and quality of the
consignment. It's always worth a try if you have other, equally
competent firms available. However, it's usually a mistake to
deal with a house of lesser quality just to save a percent or two
of commission. In auctioneering, like other things, you get what
you pay for. There may be a good reason why one house ac-
cepts lower commissions than another, and it may show up in
the quality of the auction it conducts.

Another of the money matters has to do with incidental sales
costs. You, as consignor, are generally expected to pay all—or
a portion—of such things as photography (if your pieces are
illustrated in a catalog), transportation to the auction house and
insurance while in transit. First, try to determine what these
costs or expenses will be; then see what you can do about getting

them reduced. Once a contract is signed, it's too late to complain!

The nonfinancial items of the consignment agreement—terms of sale—may, in some cases, prove as important to you as the money matters. One of these is the question of reserves. As you know, there is always a pull and tug between consignor and consignee on this issue—you want to protect your treasure from a bad day on the block; the auctioneer wants to move the goods. If you chose your auctioneer well, though, you can rely on his recommendations as to where reserves are necessary and what they should be.

Other terms of sale include the questions of when your goods are to be sold and with what other pieces. If your merchandise is of medium quality, you will want to place it in an auction with better pieces. The presence of quality will pull up the general price level. If it is of top value, you want to avoid a sale where the general level is below it. Insist, where possible, on knowing the nature of the auction in which your consignment will appear and try to get the best situation.

Also, as you can imagine, pieces which are illustrated in the sale catalog (especially on the cover) often bring premium prices. So try to negotiate for illustrations, even if you must pay a portion of the photography costs. In most cases, it will pay off. The same thing is true of advertising. The auctioneer should be able to assure you that the sale will be advertised in local, regional and, perhaps, national media. These ads usually include descriptions of the choicer lots. Try to see that something from your consignment gets into print. The more notice a piece gets, the more bidders it draws and the more likely it is to go for—or above—the high estimate.

Finally, insist on including some agreement as to how long after the sale payment will be made. In general, smaller local houses should settle their accounts within 30 days, and larger firms within 60 days. Also come to an understanding as to the disposition of goods which are not sold, either because of reserves or because they don't elicit an opening bid. Generally, such pieces should be run through another auction at the same house after the lapse of a few weeks or months; then, if they don't move, they should be transferred elsewhere for sale.

11 Dealing with Dealers

Long gone are those halcyon days at auctions when you could survey the audience with confidence, serene in the knowledge that at all but a few big city galleries, most of your competitors were local farmers and householders out for a bit of entertainment and a few minor purchases, but not interested in that brass bed or early candlestick you spotted.

Today's auction crowd, to the contrary, is generally at least 20 percent dealers. They make an impact on the market that is far in excess of their numbers. This is because dealers are serious and continual buyers. Average collectors confine themselves to several categories, at the most, and may attend several auctions to buy one or two items. Dealers, on the other hand, must buy constantly, and in great variety, in order to replenish stock as it is sold.

Many auctioneers estimate that better than 60 percent of their sales are "to the trade," and as more individuals become dealers at one level or another, the trend continues upward. Indeed, it has been said that professional buyers substantially support the auction market in many areas.

If you wonder why every obscure country auction sports a parking lot filled, even in the dead of winter, with cars licensed in Massachusetts, New York, Pennsylvania and points south, it's because you don't understand the dealer's dilemma in the present market situation. The combination of inflation and unemployment has largely cut the center out of the antiques market. Those individuals earning $12,000 to $25,000 per year who a short time ago had disposable income to spend on antiques and collectibles, are now mostly out of the market. Their place has been taken by the "high rollers," well-to-do collectors who are buying for investment and as a hedge against inflation. This kind of collector deals primarily through agents and buys the best. Middle-range objects won't do. Today, increasingly, the best is gravitating toward the auction market; and the dealers must follow it. Then, of course, their presence at the auction fans the flames of competition, and the whole process is accelerated.

Moreover, there seems to be an obsession (particularly in the large centers like New York and Boston) with obtaining and selling only newly discovered things. This so-called "fresh merch" has been off the market for various periods of time, either because it was in a private collection or because it was tucked away in some old barn. There is considerable prestige and profit in offering something that has not passed through the hands of a dozen dealers, but in today's highly competitive market, such items are hard to find. Since estates, collections and barn lots tend to end up at auction, that is where the dealers go to seek fresh merchandise.

So, accept with good grace the fact that for the foreseeable future, the man or woman bidding at your elbow is probably a dealer. (In fact, you may have one at each elbow!) However, as we have pointed out previously, if you are a knowledgeable collector, you don't need to fear the competition. While the professional's presence makes it less likely that you'll be able to "steal" an undiscovered treasure, you'll nearly always prevail. You just need to pay closer attention to what the piece is worth on the open market.

Even the dreaded "ring" (see chapter 5) should not affect you if you know values and your merchandise. The ring certainly can affect the auctioneer's profits, and those of the consignor. As a consequence, auctioneers and their consignors generally are not overly fond of rings, to say the least! When confronted with a particularly successful one, they may resort to such measures as ignoring the ring leader's bids or withdrawing from the sale those items—such as rugs or jewelry—which the ring members want. Then, of course, might come that day of which every auctioneer dreams: when two or more competing rings show up at the same auction and bid against each other! Ring operators are too smart to let that happen very often. So, in the long run, most auction houses simply accept all but the most persistent and blatant rings as a fact of business life.

Dealers, however, have an impact on the auction market which is quite apart from their rôle as buyers. Since they frequently put through auction the merchandise they regard as

Here is a detail of "Icebergs," one of the most famous paintings by Frederic Edwin Church, and lost for over 100 years. Newly discovered by Sotheby Parke Bernet experts in a home for boys in Manchester, England, the painting set a new record when it was sold at auction at Sotheby's.

unsalable in their shops, they provide the auctioneer with additional grist for his mill.

Perhaps less well known outside the trade is that certain large dealers, usually importers, provide a major portion of the objects sold at some of the regional auction houses. The process is essentially a form of consignment. The auctioneer takes a certain amount of merchandise (paintings, furniture or whatever) from the dealer, which he then sells—or attempts to sell. This material may be the "other additions" mentioned in advertising for estate sales; or, in some instances, it might make up the entire auction. If the auctioneer doesn't sell any piece, he returns it to his supplier who furnishes him with replacements while shipping the rejected piece off to another auction gallery in another area of the country for a "second try."

This system helps auction galleries in areas of the country which are starved for merchandise available for auction. The growing interest in antiques and collectibles makes for a ready market—often at prices well above those that the same merchandise could command in older, more settled regions.

In this arrangement, the dealer is compensated for his services by way of a minimum price placed on each item. A sofa, for example, is sent out under an agreement that the first $1,200 of the auction price goes to the dealer (assuring him of a good profit on his investment). If, at the auction, the piece brings $1,600, the auctioneer pockets the entire $400. Since the $1,200 figure acts as a reserve, you can be sure that the auctioneer won't ever sell the piece for less than $1,200! In itself this is a perfectly proper arrangement, but it helps to keep individual buyers from getting anything at much below market value through such a gallery.

Certain dealers have also learned to use auction houses, particularly larger ones, to establish their own markets and prices. This technique is especially prevalent in the area of fine arts, where schools and periods of painting (such as the American Impressionists), which were long ignored by collectors and critics, are now attracting renewed attention. The reason for this renewed attention, incidentally, at least in part, is that work by recognized artists has become unavailable or prohibitively expensive.

What happens is this: A sophisticated fine arts dealer locates several paintings by a competent, but largely ignored, academic artist (preferably with such credentials as membership in the National Academy or a period of study under a major painter).

The dealer buys these paintings, usually for a few thousand dollars apiece. Then he puts one of them up for auction with a respectable house, often paying a premium for advertising and color illustration. When the work is auctioned off, the dealer's agents in the audience run the price up among themselves to some agreed-upon figure, say $30,000.

At this point, the innocent auctioneer may become a bit suspicious. Here is a piece selling so far above estimate, perhaps even setting a world auction record for that particular painter —yet the artist is totally unknown! Still, such records are regarded as a distinction for the gallery when they are achieved, so the auctioneer will probably swallow his doubts and make a note to keep his eye out for other work by the artist.

The wily dealer, on the other hand, having just paid $30,000 for his own painting, will apply the auction standard to the other paintings by this artist in his possession. He now has three or four $30,000 paintings to offer to the public and a world-record auction price to support his prices for this painter's work.

This technique is very effective in creating a private market as well as inflated dealer prices, but it doesn't necessarily guarantee that the next time a piece by this artist goes on the block it will bring a comparable price—or even a much higher estimate. In fact, Nancy Druckman of Sotheby Parke Bernet states that as far as her firm is concerned, even a world record price would not cause them to increase their estimates substantially where the artist involved was obscure and had never brought a comparable price. Sotheby Parke Bernet would look, rather, for a "track record," a series of high prices to show real collector interest in the paintings. In order to achieve this, of course, our dealer might have to buy several of his paintings at auction, an expensive business. He will probably be content with what he has already achieved: namely, the establishment of a recognized and current auction price which he can use to advertise the paintings he owns.

While some dealers are using auctions to "make a market," others are using them to "protect" theirs. Let's assume that you are a dealer who owns a group of prints which you price and sell at $700 apiece. If you learn that similar work by the same artist is being offered at auction, you are likely to appear at the sale (or rather, your representative will) to bid these examples up to somewhere near the level of those you're selling in your shop. You usually don't want the prints (if you're not careful you may get stuck with them), but you certainly don't want clients to come into your store and tell you that they have just seen prints "exactly like yours" go for half the price at such-and-such auction gallery. In this case, you're just protecting your investment.

Now, of course, much of this will have more impact on your auction-going if you happen to own an oil by that obscure painter whose work has just brought $30,000. But even if you never heard of him, it does point out that the rôle of auction gallery as an establisher of market prices must be taken with a small grain of salt. Like all markets, this one can be manipulated—by rings, by consignors, by dealers.

12 How to Become an Auctioneer

The superstar of the auction house is the auctioneer. Standing high above the audience with hundreds of eyes riveted on his or her every move, the auctioneer is always the center of attention. Moreover, if he is good, the auction process—the mundane process of buying and selling—becomes a form of exciting theater. Gesturing broadly as he describes his offerings, joking and bantering with the onlookers, he catches and holds their attention. The mesmerizing bidding chant begins: He draws his bids, here one, there another, attempting to create rivalries, to incite desire and, most important, to convince everyone out there in that vast sea of faces that not only is the piece on sale wonderful and well worth the bids, but that each and every one has a chance to possess it—and at a song!

In a multi-million dollar business, at a time when auction proceeds are commonly counted in the tens of thousands of dollars, the auctioneer can become a superstar, particularly in the media-conscious art and antiques world. But there is an old saying in the trade: "An auctioneer is only as good as his next sale"; and everyone in the field is aware of the fact that hard work and knowledge keep the best on top.

It's an exciting and profitable occupation, and one which, oddly enough, is not yet overcrowded. Moreover, it's a field distinctly open to women as well as men, and more women are entering it every day.

Breaking into the auction world isn't all that hard. Most people start out by approaching a local auctioneer for a job as a clerk or handler. Of course, you don't make all that much money, but you get invaluable experience. Then, after a year or two in the business, you can go out on your own with some confidence of an open-ended future. In this, as in most private enterprise, your ultimate earnings are limited only by your abilities.

The National Auctioneers' Association, a professional group (composed of the most experienced auctioneers), estimates that there are some 25,000 licensed auctioneers active in the United States. The term "license" should be qualified, though, since laws vary greatly from state to state. Some require you to pass a qualifying examination. Others insist you post a monetary bond, and in other states all you need to do to enter the business is pay a small fee and set up shop. While there's no evidence that the incidence of auction abuse is higher in the "loosely licensed" states, the trend is toward more formal licensing and increased government control—a mixed blessing—but inevitable.

The 20 or so states which license auctioneers pattern their laws, for the most part, on those of Indiana, and call for a period of on-the-job training, a written examination and some inquiry into the applicant's background and character.

The National Auctioneers' Association, and leading members of the trade, actively support setting up uniform licensing rules as a means of raising standards and public confidence.

With uniform licensing requirements, if you were an auctioneer licensed to do business in one state for a period of time, you could be licensed in other states without further testing. This system, which has existed for years among lawyers and doctors, is becoming a necessity as auction houses range far afield in search of business.

But, of course, a prerequisite to any sort of licensing is training and practical experience. The auctioneers' craft is a complex one, encompassing far more than surface theatrics. To be a professional you must know your merchandise and how to obtain it. You must understand the secrets of salesmanship and group psychology, must be able to carry vast amounts of information in your head and recall them instantly while under the pressure of a frenetic auction sale. You should also be a competent, organized businessperson, have some knowledge of accounting and law as they apply to the auction field and be able to deal with a variety of governmental regulatory agencies. None of this expertise comes easily. Learning it takes time and effort.

Not so long ago, this learning took place almost entirely through one of the few remaining apprentice systems. If you were seeking to enter the field you began as a typist, clerk or handler. You swept floors, typed letters, packed and unpacked

At the venerable Missouri Auction School in Kansas City, a neophyte, training to become an auctioneer, handles the mike.

consignments, answered the telephone and assisted in displaying pieces as they were auctioned off. As your knowledge grew you'd be given greater responsibility. You might be sent out to look at merchandise offered for consignment—place a price on it and, perhaps, even make the decision on whether or not to accept it for the gallery. You would also begin to appear at pre-sale viewings where you would answer visitors' questions and do the sort of legitimate "puffing" which can be crucial to the prices obtained at auction. And, most of all, you'd learn by observation. As one current auction "biggie" put it:

"If your boss was good, you knew it; and you wanted, naturally, to find out how he got that way. Now, some of the old timers were—and are—pretty tight-lipped. They saw all of us helpers as potential competitors somewhere down the road, and they weren't about to give anything away—least of all really good stuff like where they got things or that special list of collectors and dealers that they called when certain items were going on the block.

"The man I started out with wasn't like that. He was always ready to offer advice or answer questions, and he seemed to take a lot of pride in the number of his ex-employees who became successful in the business.

"On the other hand, even the tight-lipped ones couldn't stop you from watching and listening when they were in action, and that was very important. It was, in fact, sort of like the old log with the teacher on one end and the student on the other. There weren't any books. In fact, there still isn't a real primer for the beginning auctioneer; but every veteran is a walking encyclopedia of the trade. He seldom does things just by chance, so you could learn a lot by just watching and trying to figure what he's up to.

"For example, my boss would sometimes give a fast knock to some bidder—really let him have a good buy. It took me a long time to figure out why he was doing that. Then, I began to notice something. The people who got those fast knocks were also usually the ones who got the bidding going when no one else wanted to open on a piece. It wasn't collusion or anything like that. These were customers who liked my boss and wanted to be helpful. He appreciated that; and he, in turn, would give them a good deal whenever he could. It's relationships like that, which take years to build, that really set the veteran auctioneer apart."

This sort of informal training is still the heart of the auction business. Larger houses, such as Christie's and Sotheby Parke

Bernet have formalized the process by introducing classes more appropriate to their primarily college trained personnel; but the basic principles remain. You learn by watching and listening, then doing. In England and Europe, this process is carried to the extreme. You may assist in a shop or gallery for 5 to 10 years before you're allowed to assume real responsibility or to call an auction. In the United States, on the other hand, the person who sweeps your floor today may be running his or her own auction down the road next month.

But the auction field is becoming so vast and its requirements so complex, that increasingly, neophytes are turning to some form of academic training At present, less than a dozen schools of auctioneering are scattered about the country. Typically they enroll about 50 students each, in semiannual sessions which last from one to two weeks and try to cover all aspects of the business. They pay specific attention to specialties such as real estate, antiques and livestock auctions. For faculty, they draw upon leading auctioneers, as well as specialists in related fields such as law and accounting.

The oldest of these schools is the Missouri Auction School in Kansas City. It started out training livestock auctioneers at a time when that branch of the craft was central to the whole auctioneering world. However, over the course of the past decade, corporate and government involvement in the livestock field have made the auctioneer's rôle less important. On the other hand, greatly increased interest in antiques and collectibles has led to a demand for more people trained in estate and general auctions. Consequently, Missouri, along with the southern schools which once emphasized tobacco sales training, diversified its program. Today the goal of all auctioneering schools is to produce a well-rounded professional, capable of dealing with any sale presented to him.

As an example of the "bill of fare" offered at such institutions, the Jim Graham School in Florida supplements basic courses like "The Professional Auction Chant" and "How To Determine Values" with more esoteric classes such as: "Bidders' Body Language" and "True Self Confidence." The International Auction School in Massachusetts, which emphasizes training in the areas of house and estate sales and, especially, antiques (the school president, Douglas Bilodeau, refers to his curriculum as "boot camp" for the antiques field), gives a background in the basics of the business. The school offers courses such as "Clerking and Cashiering," "Estate Liquidations" and "Sales Management,"

Douglas Bilodeau, of the Douglas Galleries, with hammer poised, is about to "knock down" a lot. Once the hammer falls, the sale on that particular lot is completed.

Courtesy Missouri Auction School

"What am I bid?" At the Mis-
souri Auction School, class is in
session.

but also teaches "The Art of Salesmanship" and "Self Confidence." Other institutions such as Repperts of Decatur, Indiana and New Jersey's Career Institute School of Auctioneering combine the traditional training in the auction chant with up-to-date information on how to deal with the Internal Revenue Service, keep business records and handle client problems.

Most schools offer and emphasize a course on "ethics," the moral and fiduciary responsibilities of the auction house employee.

Though all auction schools make an effort to place their graduates with galleries or auction houses, administrators find that many students come to them with some previous experience and the specific goal of running their own businesses. It's not unusual, they say, for a man or woman fresh out of auctioneering school to call an auction. On the other hand, not all advance as rapidly as one of Douglas Bilodeau's students who celebrated his graduation by grossing $140,000 on his first trip to the podium!

Auction houses which concentrate on fine arts and antiques have another source of employees. For years, gallery owners like C. B. Charles have been recruiting bright college graduates with fine arts degrees and an interest in the antiques business. Such undergraduate education provides some background, but hardly equips students to deal with the practicalities of day-to-day business.

On the other hand, during the past 10 years, universities have begun to offer graduate courses in museum sciences and American studies, and graduates of these programs are proving apt candidates for the auction market. The Delaware University program, operated in conjunction with the Henry Francis du Pont Winterthur Museum, is well known, as are the comparable programs offered at Cooperstown, New York, and through Yale University. Though these programs are mostly directed toward Americana, they train their graduates in such areas as conservation and the recognition of fakes and reproductions, both extremely important aspects of the auctioneer's training.

Interestingly enough, the auction community also has a graduate school. In 1976, the National Auctioneers' Association, in conjunction with Indiana University, established the Certified Auctioneers' Education Institute, which offers a series of three yearly courses on the University campus. This program is limited to practicing auctioneers with at least two years' experience and is designed to broaden the student's professional background.

On these two pages, a "pro" in action. Douglas Bilodeau of the Douglas Galleries wields his hammer, waves his hand, cajoles, beckons (and sometimes even browbeats) his audience into bigger bidding.

Upon completion of the program, an auctioneer becomes eligible for full membership in the C.A.E.I.

And you can even go abroad to study. London's Sotheby Parke Bernet Gallery offers a year-long course in auction skills which is particularly helpful if you're interested in working at a large international gallery. However, the cost of attendance is substantial, and satisfactory completion does not assure a job with Sotheby's.

Other, less formal, educational experiences are provided by the various state auctioneers' associations and by the National Auctioneers' Association, which also sponsors semiannual conferences.

With these educational programs, the traditional image of the auctioneer as a bellowing master of gamesmanship is gradually being replaced with that of the multi-faceted professional, adept in a variety of fields and perfectly capable of dealing as an equal with businessmen, accountants and bankers. And yet, the field remains one of the last great frontiers of economic opportunity. Douglas Bilodeau declares flatly ". . . there is no other area of American business where the individual with minimum financial backing, minimum formal education and minimum experience can get ahead so quickly." Not all the gold in the auction house is in the jewelry lots!

13 Behind the Scenes at a Major Firm

For most of us, the auctioneer is the whole story. Other people—handlers, clerks, and the like—are of only peripheral importance. How all that merchandise gets to the house and gets sold remains pretty much of a mystery. Yet, if you really want to understand the auction process and use your knowledge in buying or selling, it's important to know all about it.

How a gallery is run may depend upon its size, sales emphasis, the clientele it serves and other factors. However, we can draw some generalizations, and in order to illustrate them, we'll examine three important American auction houses. Each one is a leader in its field, and each one does its job in a different way. In this chapter we will discuss Sotheby Parke Bernet, a firm of world-wide stature. In another chapter we will turn our attention to regional and itinerant houses.

Founded in 1744, and with offices in London, New York, Zurich, Toronto and Los Angeles, Sotheby Parke Bernet is the world's largest auction house. Its New York City office consists of a main building on Madison Avenue, and a second gallery, known as P.B. 84, on 84th Street. Together, they handle over 200 auction sales a year, both in-house and on site (at the place where the merchandise is located).

Sotheby's consists of no less than 36 distinct departments, each with a head or director, and a group of assistants. As the firm sells material in every area of fine art and antiques, these divisions range from such obvious classifications as Chinese Art and Contemporary Paintings to esoterica like Vintage Cars and Paper Weights.

Finer things, important paintings and sculpture, pre-1850 furnishings and the like, are sold at the main gallery. P.B. 84

specializes in late 19th- and early 20th-century decorative arts, as well as collectors' items, such as dolls and beer steins.

Over 600 individuals are employed at Sotheby Parke Bernet, performing functions as diverse as maintenance man, accountant and appraiser. The key to the whole operation, however, is the professional staff—men and women, most of whom are fine arts graduates, who are trained to find, evaluate and sell the thousands of items which, each year, pass through the company's hands. All candidates for these positions take part in a rigorous training program lasting a year, and consisting of graded daily class work and research projects.

One of the most important aspects of the new employee's job is the procuring of saleable merchandise. Competition for quality antiques and art has never been keener, and even Sotheby Parke Bernet, with its vast network of overseas and American offices, must aggressively seek out consignments.

Sotheby does this in a variety of ways. As the best-known of all North American auction houses, it is approached regularly by estate lawyers, banks and wealthy individuals seeking to dispose of valuables. These contacts are of great importance, but the firm has also developed ways of reaching those who might not normally call or come in. One of these is its appraisal program.

If you have an item you'd like to have evaluated you may call the New York gallery, to set up an appointment to meet with a member of an appropriate department who will either appraise it orally without charge or, for a nominal fee, issue a written appraisal. While such an evaluation implies no obligation on either side, inevitably some of the appraised items will be consigned.

Along with this program, Sotheby Parke Bernet instituted its Heirloom Discovery Days some six years ago. Under this arrangement, a group of three or four house experts will go anywhere in the country to conduct appraisals, usually under the auspices of a local charitable organization which collects a small fee for the service. So far, the firm has run these sessions in over 100 different cities and has turned up such interesting finds as a porcelain Medici bowl valued at $180,000 and a fourteenth century Russian icon worth $30,000. Again, many of the objects they appraise are later consigned.

Finally, as do smaller auction houses, Sotheby Parke Bernet just "noses out" goods. Its staff answers letters and telephone calls and travels to the far ends of the land on "house calls" to examine merchandise.

Courtesy Sotheby Parke Bernet

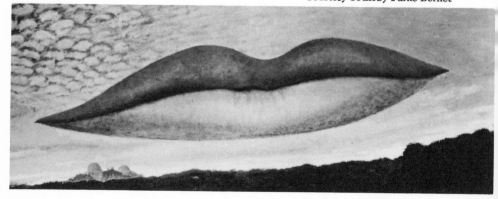

Finding auctionable goods is just the beginning, important as it is. Once the merchandise is located, the firm must strike a bargain for the consignment (Sotheby Parke Bernet does not buy goods on its own behalf), and enter into a formal contract. Normally, this covers the firm's commission (10 percent is standard, six percent from dealers), transportation charges, insurance, photography, and so on. All these items are negotiable.

Once the details are completed, the merchandise, if it is small or consists of just a few pieces, is shipped directly to the New York office. If the collection is substantial or consists of sizable objects, such as furniture or automobiles, Sotheby's dispatches one or more of its staff to inventory the consignment on the premises.

This inventory, like those conducted by most auctioneers—though perhaps a bit more elaborate—is handled in the following manner. A description of each lot (which may consist of one or several objects) is entered on an individual tally sheet. The sheets are then arranged in categories; rugs, for example, are grouped together. The sale is then "laid out" from these sheets; the order determined with the goal of creating interest in and generating great value from each item. Once the layout is completed, the lots are numbered, usually from lot #1 on, so that the catalog may be prepared.

The question of layout or sale sequence is of fundamental concern for every auctioneer. In each consignment, be it at Sotheby's or the humblest of local galleries, there are some good things and some not so good. If the sale is extensive

(Opposite page, top) "El Dorado" by Henri de Toulouse-Lautrec sold for $26,000, a record for a poster. (Left) "A L'Heure de l'Observatoire: Les Amoureux" by Man Ray for $750,000, record Surrealist painting.

Here, at one of Sotheby Parke Bernet's "Heirloom Discovery"

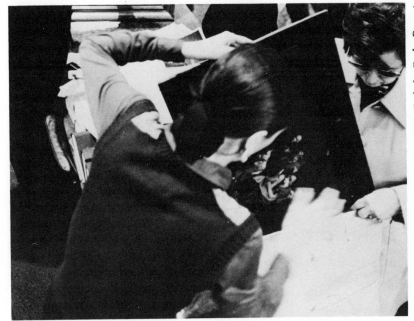

Courtesy Sotheby Parke Bernet

days, staff members volunteer to examine family "heirlooms."

enough, there may also be groupings by type—a dozen cast-iron banks, for example—that naturally go together and will probably attract a set of competing bidders.

Most sales are built around a collection of choice pieces, valuable in their own right for historical or artistic reasons. These items will attract potential buyers and, hopefully, will set the "tone" for the sale. So important are these "leaders" that a gallery will often acquire them on consignment, at terms extremely favorable to the owner (such as little or no commission), simply because their presence will so enhance the sale that the house will make an ample profit from the other, lesser things in the catalog.

Since the order in which choice pieces appear in the sale may substantially affect all the prices, the auctioneer's job is to figure out the winning combination. The usual practice is as follows: The best pieces are never placed at the beginning or end of the show. Too many people come and go at those times. Generally, the star-quality material will be found 15 or 20 lots into the sale, and it will be followed closely by comparable but lesser items. The theory is that the best example (particularly if it was advertised and illustrated in the catalog) will bring out a group of competitive bidders. They will battle for it, pushing the price to a high figure and, equally important, establishing a general feeling of value for all similar examples yet to come. The underbidders, their funds still available, since they failed to capture the top prize, will be able to pursue its lesser relatives, serene in the knowledge that if Item A went for that much, surely Items B, C and even D are of almost equal value.

Close relatives to the cataloging "family" are the questions of estimates and reserves. Estimates will be of great interest to you if you are a potential consignor. You may even decide to choose one auction house over another on the basis of which one puts the highest estimate on your wares. However, you're counting your sales before they "hatch." By its very nature, an estimate can never be more than an informed guess as to what a piece will bring at auction. Perhaps the most realistic, as well as the most humorous, statement about estimates appears in the front of each sale catalog issued by Maine's Barridoff Galleries: "Estimates are intended only as the loosest possible guideline and should be read with a fair amount of amusement."

That does not mean, though, that they are applied without consideration. Quite the contrary is the case. At Sotheby Parke Bernet, the staff pores over prior sales records (their own and,

where available, those of competitors) in an attempt to determine the "track record" of every piece. Once it obtains the
figures, the staff adjusts them to reflect such factors as how long
ago the piece was sold, the quality of this specimen as opposed
to those previously offered, the trends in the field, and so forth.
Eventually they come up with figures, the high and low estimates, and Sotheby Parke Bernet reports that 90 percent of the
time its lots sell at—or above—the low estimate. Consignors
seldom complain if the price exceeds the high estimate! Still,
evaluation always poses a problem for the auction house employee. As Nancy Druckman of Sotheby Parke Bernet's Americana Division expresses it:

"One of the problems of being in the auction business is that
we have to provide our customers with responsible auction
estimates, but if you overestimate, you may make it difficult to
attract bidders."

And, of course, estimates which are too low (though, perhaps
realistic) may discourage potential consignors. Talk about tough
choices; it's between Scylla and Charybdis!

Another important function of the estimate (other than providing a bidder with some idea of what a piece will go for) is
that the reserve is based on it. While many auctions are entirely
or largely unreserved, there is a clear trend toward placing
minimum prices on the better items. Auction gallery reserves—
and policies regarding them—vary greatly. At Sotheby Parke
Bernet the usual reserve is two-thirds of the low estimate. Never
will a reserve exceed the high estimate, and only rarely will
they permit one above the low estimate. Since the reserve is a
confidential matter between the consignor and the house, the
would-be buyer will never know the exact amount, but it helps
to understand what you're up against.

While all these decisions and calculations are being made,
other, more mundane, matters must be dealt with. The consignment is carefully packed and then shipped (by a professional
concern familiar with the handling of art and antiques) from
the owner's home to the Sotheby Parke Bernet gallery.

When the shipment arrives in the gallery, at least three
months prior to sale date, it is unpacked, again by specially
trained personnel, photographed when appropriate, and the
photos matched to the catalog descriptions.

Sotheby Parke Bernet, in common with most sizable galleries,
has an extensive public relations department and makes a great
effort to advertise each sale extensively and well in advance.

Some three weeks prior to the auction, the catalog goes to press. Weeks or even months before the date of the sale, notices of the auction begin to appear in antiques and arts trade publications, and in the final week, newspaper advertising will also be used.

During the last few days prior to the sale, the items are placed on view in the firm's galleries, and members of the staff are available to discuss estimates and answer questions about the merchandise.

At Sotheby's, sales are conducted by a team of auctioneers. Division heads and higher-ups may even appear if the quality of the material warrants it. Auctions are generally conducted before a packed house, their pace quickened by an electronic "scoreboard" which records bids in several languages and currencies. At particularly important sales where it's impossible to accommodate all bidders in the main hall, closed-circuit television cameras are used to service crowds in other areas.

After the sale, it's the purchasers' responsibility to remove their acquisitions from the premises, though Sotheby Parke Bernet, like other large auctioneers, will arrange transportation at the buyer's expense.

Of course, the conclusion of the sale does not bring an end to the gallery's responsibilities. The last phase of the operation —making payment—is, from the point of view of the consignor, the most important. At Sotheby's an entire division, "Settlements," is devoted to this task, delivering checks and statements to consignors within 35 days of sale.

This sort of efficiency is the hallmark of the large firm. With an enormous volume of merchandise and a great number of consignors and buyers, such houses must, of necessity, develop a highly systematized approach. In the process, you lose something of the close, personal relationship possible in smaller galleries, but you gain accessibility to a vast market and a high degree of professionalism.

14 Regional and Roving Houses

Sotheby Parke Bernet, Christie's, Phillips and the other large, international galleries are not typical auction houses, and most American auction buffs have little—or no—contact with them. Much more common is a firm like Douglas Galleries of South Deerfield, Massachusetts. Located in a thriving auction area, Douglas is a "full service gallery." That is, it sells not just the art and antiques from an estate or household, but also nearly anything else, from used furniture to farm implements—plus the house itself!

The firm receives enough merchandise to hold 60 to 70 auctions a year and to gross close to a million dollars a year without, for the most part, going outside the New England area. In fact, most consignors live within 50 miles of South Deerfield. This is a far cry from Sotheby Parke Bernet and its international clientele.

Like its larger counterparts, the Douglas firm relies primarily on consignments. It owns outright only 10 percent of the merchandise which it offers. Consignments are obtained through the usual sources—private agents, banks, lawyers and the like—but Douglas Bilodeau, president of the firm, prefers referrals from satisfied consignors and buyers. These can be an important source of new business.

Despite the number of auctions it runs each year, Douglas Galleries operates with a staff of only 6 full-time employees, plus 8 to 10 part-timers. If you call the office, likely as not, you'll be connected directly with the president, himself! No elaborate departmental structure exists, such as at Christie's or Sotheby Parke Bernet, and training is strictly on-the-job. People with an interest in the auction world "walk in the door,"

140

and in time, under the guidance of Bilodeau's staff, become knowledgeable.

Since neither overhead nor the nature of the items justify it, the gallery seldom issues an elaborate catalog. This is usually the case with smaller regional auction houses; nonillustrated, mimeographed sheets are generally the most that supplements the auctioneer's verbal descriptions. In other ways, though, Douglas Galleries conforms closely to the procedures adopted by larger houses. Consignments are carefully handled and inventoried, reserves are established, where necessary, and the goods are sold with a flair born of years in the business.

Perhaps the greatest difference (other than the obvious one of dollar volume) between small firms, such as this one, and the national or international houses, has to do with client relations. At Sotheby Parke Bernet, the average buyer knows no one on the staff, personally. Only the most active attendees can claim more than a nodding relationship with department heads. At Douglas, on the other hand, if you attend regularly (you need not buy) you become a part of the family, and you're greeted and catered to with warmth and friendliness.

Another type of company, quite different from the local or regional firm, which rests on the sound base of community patronage, is the itinerant or "roving" auction house. One of the leading businesses in this category is C. B. Charles Galleries of Pontiac, Michigan. Charles conducts 20 to 30 auction sales a year, and 90 percent of these are held outside Pontiac. This travel does not imply, as it would with Sotheby Parke Bernet or Douglas, that the auctions are conducted on site for the sake of convenience or because of the historical importance or "star" quality of the location. Quite the contrary. C. B. Charles conducts his sales in quality hotels and motels with merchandise transported from his storerooms in Michigan. In this way, the company brings high quality auctions to areas of the country where there are only a limited number of such sales.

Unlike the other firms we have just discussed, at least 50 percent of the current Charles Galleries inventory is the result of outright purchases (the proprietor specializes in buying the estates of prominent people like Judy Garland and Douglas Fairbanks). Such gallery-owned goods are carefully blended with consignments in an effort to achieve an attractive and balanced selection of merchandise.

Also, auctions run by the Charles firm are specifically directed at the retail, rather than the wholesale, trade. Where a given

A rural house sale in central Missouri. At the moment, a chair is being auctioned off. Next could be the washer/dryer or even the bed! Note the ever-present cowboy hat, auction trademark in the South and the Midwest.

At an outdoor southern auction weather can determine success.

sale at Sotheby's or Douglas may result in as high as 60 percent
dealer purchases, the figure is usually less than 20 percent at
Charles.

This emphasis on the collector is reflected in several policies
of the firm which are not typical of auction houses in general.
In the first place, most sales are "by request"; that means that,
rather than calling out merchandise in numerical or catalog
order, pieces are sold as the customers direct. You simply pick
up a request slip at the door and indicate the numbers of pieces
you want called. If you've ever waited hours for a chance to bid
on a desired object, you can appreciate how welcome this innovation is. It is also helpful to the auctioneer. He catalogs more
items than he could ever sell in the allotted time, his clientele
can pick and choose among his numerous wares—and he's
assured of opening bids from them.

A second Charles device seldom encountered elsewhere is
the auction by invitation. Rather than publicly advertising a
sale, the gallery sends flyers to its extensive mailing list, offering
patrons an opportunity to bid exclusively.

As a further service to the collector or to the private investor,

A *midwestern "on premises" auction on lawn. Note lot held up.*

Charles Galleries catalogs (all sales are by catalog) contain more detailed descriptions than is usual. Often they are color-coded to enable bidders to locate specific subjects quickly, such as china or bronzes. Often the auctioneer will add to these descriptions orally to make clear the significance of a given object.

The nature of the business of the itinerant auctioneer creates problems not usually faced by the gallery which conducts most of its sales at home. Most obvious is the packing and transportation of thousands of fragile and costly objects. Charles has devised a system involving custom-made, compartmented trucks to prevent shifting and to allow for packing by category. Room dividers and showcases are mounted on wheels and transported in the trucks, so that they may be rolled in and out of the set-up area; so are space-saving, square storage barrels. Perhaps, the most clever innovation is a vacuum cleaner-like device which blows Styrofoam pellets into the packing boxes as they are loaded, and sucks them out again as the goods are removed. With this equipment, and a highly trained road crew, Charles can set up or dismantle an auction room in less than eight hours!

C. B. Charles Galleries is staffed by some 20 people, most of whom have been with the firm for at least 10 years. As with Douglas, they are chiefly trained on-the-job. The usual process is for beginners to start working on a part-time basis and then to graduate into a full-time position. There is no true departmental division in the firm other than such areas as accounting and advertising, and most employees are expected to be familiar with a full line of fine arts and antiques. Charles does not auction household goods and things of that nature.

The firm obtains some of its merchandise through house calls and some through its appraisal services, but the bulk of its items are obtained through the efforts of agents. These are people employed in related fields, such as banking and accounting, who watch for available art and antiques, and either inform Charles or act on its behalf. Every auction house employs agents, and usually they are rewarded for their services by receipt of a fixed percentage (usually one to four percent) of the price which their "finds" bring at auction. This sum is paid out of the auctioneer's share of the proceeds. Unlike many other firms, though, Charles pays the "finder's fee" in advance, a practice which the proprietor feels leads to better relationships with his agents.

Like most sophisticated auction galleries, C. B. Charles uses a computerized settlement system and is able to make payment to consignors within 17 to 20 days of sale. The firm also employs other technical innovations, such as the use of color slides projected on an eight-by-eight screen to show auction goods too large to fit into the selling space.

Though Sotheby Parke Bernet, Douglas and Charles differ— and often rather substantially in their methods of operation, scope and clientele—in many ways they are quite similar. This is so much the case, in fact, that if you are an observant auction goer who takes the trouble to study how your local gallery functions, you should be in an excellent position to determine what is going on and, therefore, what is influencing prices in most houses anywhere in the country.

But, beyond this, it's important to develop a personal relationship with staff members at any auction gallery where you buy frequently. There is absolutely nothing like having a friend on the inside!

15 Discovering the European Markets

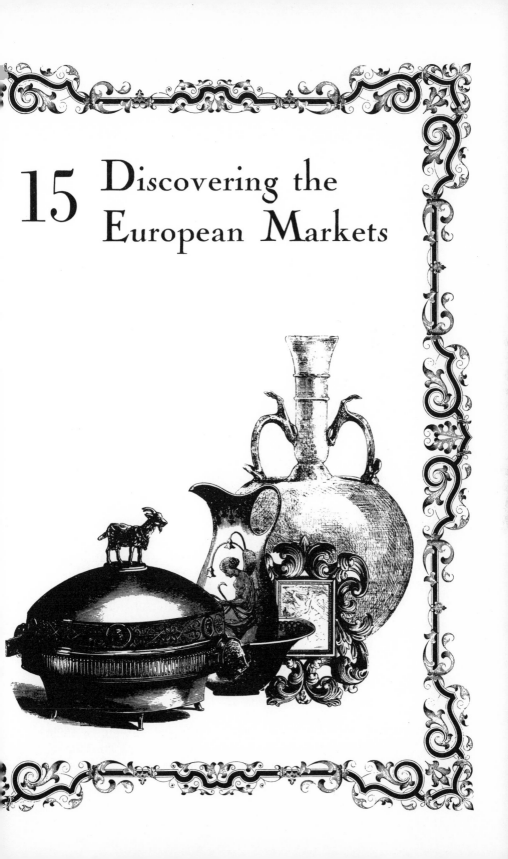

If you travel to Europe, you'll find that the auction business is well established—particularly in England, France and Holland. Bidding and other procedures may differ somewhat, but the system remains essentially the same. And, needless to say, there is a vast amount of merchandise from which to choose.

You may feel particularly at home in the British Isles, where a common language and an identical auction system allow you to move right into the action. Auction sales are held throughout England, and some of the provincial auctions are of high quality. However, the major galleries are in London. It was there that British sales got under way back in 1676 when one William Cooper held a book auction.

It seems, in fact, that most early auctioneers sold books until the appearance on the scene in 1776 of Samuel Paterson, who founded the firm later known as Stevens' Auction Rooms. Paterson was the first to produce good quality classified catalogs of the lots being offered. Though he, too, started out as a bookseller, he soon began to sell other things. Some of these were unique, to say the least. In the 1830s, Paterson offered such oddments as the shrunken, tattooed head of a Maori chieftain (it brought about $3), the mummy of a sacred Egyptian cat (a bargain at 90¢), and "the identical prayer book used by Charles I on the scaffold with his name written in his own handwriting in the middle of the book." The prayer book was clearly well appreciated, bringing some $250, a substantial sum in those days.

Not all the rarities offered at Stevens' fared so well. In 1829, the firm sold from the "miscellaneous curiosities of Dr. Clarke, the Traveler," a small box claimed to be "the box of alabaster

148

mentioned in Matthew which was brought by Mary Magdalene, filled with sweet ointment for anointing the feet of our Savior." It would appear that there was some doubt as to the provenance of this particular lot. It brought only a minuscule bid with the auctioneer noting, "A lamentable lack of appreciation for this relic was displayed by a winning bid of half a crown."

Undaunted by such setbacks, the firm moved into the 1840s with a whole new panorama of sales, embracing: shells, insects (including rare butterflies), orchids, roses, bulbs, songbirds and insects. In the early 1850s, Stevens offered the first egg of the Great Auk, a bird which became extinct less than a decade before. During the next half century, most of the 80 or so remaining Auk eggs passed through the firm's sales.

It was also in the 1850s that Stevens' inaugerated its auctions of live animals, One of the first of these was described in the November 11, 1855 issue of *Punch* by a correspondent who noted that:

> We do not quite understand how the sale is to be managed or how Mr. Stevens of King Street proposes to knock down the elephant . . . We should not be surprised if while the auctioneer is soliciting advances upon the Tiger, the Tiger were to make a sudden and unexpected advance upon the audience; and there are some lots that will hardly be under sufficient restraint to enable the porters to display them.

These problems not withstanding, the sale proceeded, and it was a success, with the elephant bringing nearly $1,000 and the dreaded tiger another $200.

There were other great nineteenth-century London auction galleries, but wars, fires and financial collapses led to the demise of most. Preeminent among the survivors are Sotheby's (known in the United States as Sotheby Parke Bernet), Christie's and Phillips. All three do a multimillion dollar annual business and have established branches in various countries throughout the world.

Sotheby's was established in 1774 by Samuel Baker, whose first gallery was on Russell Street in Covent Garden. The firm has had various principals over the years, and has been known since 1924 as Sotheby & Co., even though the last partner of that name died back in 1861. Though it, too, started out auctioning books, Sotheby's was the first English house to sell fine art. Its early book auctions were outstanding, however, with the collections of such famous personages as Napoleon, Talleyrand and the King of Holland passing through its hands.

Courtesy Christie's

The Van Gogh (opposite), "Le Jardin du Poète," from the Ford collection, sold for $5,200,000 and (above) Van Gogh's "Restaurant à Asnières" sold for $790,000. Fine art is expensive!

After 1900, antiques and fine arts became the core of the business. Today, Sotheby's is, without question, the world's leading auction house.

A worthy rival, however, is Christy, Manson & Woods, more familiarly known as Christie's. Established in 1763, Christie's first had rooms on the Pall Mall, but later moved to King Street, where it was destroyed by bombs during World War II and later rebuilt in its present form.

James Christie, founder of the firm, was a close friend of such well-known English painters as Joshua Reynolds and Thomas Gainsborough. With their assistance, he established early prominance in the field of fine arts auctioning. Large numbers of important European paintings have been handled by this gallery. Of course, Christie's has had its disappointments, too. Back in 1767 the gallery sold a religious ornament once owned by Mary Queen of Scots and given by her to a lady-in-waiting just prior to Mary's execution. Since the piece was encrusted with rubies and emeralds, the firm anticipated a high price. Unfortunately, in those days many people assumed that the relics of such ill-fated royalty were cursed and would bring nothing but bad luck. The result was a winning bid of only $60!

There are other fine London auction galleries, but don't pass up the smaller firms located outside the metropolitan area. Also active are small London firms whose advertisements appear regularly in the city newspapers, and which often offer bargains not to be found in the larger houses.

When you buy in England, anticipate paying a Value Added Tax (V.A.T.). However, you can avoid this by having your goods mailed directly to your home. Another tax-avoidance technique is to show your passport at the time of payment and get a certificate of exportation. Though the gallery collects the tax at time of payment, it will refund it by mail when you send back the receipt of the certificate signed by customs officials. (This signature proves you and your purchase have left England and releases the gallery to pay you back.)

Australia is a lesser-known but nevertheless thriving auction market. Bidding is in the English manner and the reserve system is observed here, too. A wide variety of items are sold— from heavy equipment and household goods to antiques and

Sotheby Parke Bernet (opposite) was established in 1774 and is now the world's leading firm, with many European branches.

paintings. General auctions are held once or twice a week; specialized sales (i.e., paintings) are held a few times a year. Several medium-sized houses to try are: Joel's and Aingers (Melbourne), G. K. Gray, J. R. Lawson, and F. R. Strange (Sydney). All auctioneers are licensed. In New South Wales and Western Australia, auctioneers take a qualifying course at a technical college for membership in the Auctioneer & Agents Association. In other areas, a license is provided upon submission of an application, and training is in-house.

When you go to Australia, check the local city newspapers—auction houses advertise their sales (either in-house or on-site) right before the weekend. Since country auctions selling antiques and second-hand goods abound, keep alert for informal notices. This country loves auctions, so you should be able to find one suited to your tastes within a few days of arrival.

But before moving on to other far points, this extract from an article entitled "What Is An Auctioneer?" in the *New South Wales Auctioneers and Valuers Association Bulletin* must be savored:

> As for the individual who wishes to become an Auctioneer he must above all, have a genuine flair for his chosen profession. He must start from the beginning and learn the A.B.C. of it from "A to Z" and "Z to A." He must realise that six months does not complete his training. I have been in my business since 1912, as Office Boy, Junior Storeman, Storeman, Clerk, Cashier, Bookkeeper, etc., until I first sold in 1920. I have been selling and valueing ever since and I am *still* learning. An Auctioneer can have no favorites . . . and if he is wise he will have no collection of Art Effects, Silver, Pictures, etc. Perhaps a few good pieces here and there in his home, but no collection. Remember, he is selling to the Public . . . and the Public get peculiar ideas.

The French auction system, which ranks second in importance to that of England, differs from it greatly. Before taking part, you need to be aware of certain restrictions which may affect your ability to purchase and remove lots from the country.

In the first place, the right to sell at auction in France has been owned by the central government for hundreds of years, and a variety of laws spell out how, when and where sales may be conducted. Moreover, since the privilege of running auctions belongs to the state, the government also has the authority to delegate this power to private persons and has been doing so for a long time. As far back as the reign of Louis XIV, regulations were established under which individuals could buy, for a lump sum payment, the right or license to conduct auctions in a given location. As astonishing as it may seem, these rules have been modified only once since then—during the time of Napoleon I— and they remain substantially unchanged today!

The auctioneering privilege, known in France as the *chargé*, is recognized under French law as a valuable property right; and it may be sold or willed to a descendant. It may not, however, be transferred to a non-Frenchman. Local law forbids the conducting of auctions by noncitizens.

In Paris, which is exceeded in importance as an auction center only by New York and London, there are some 300 holders of the *chargé*. About 200 more operate in other areas of the country, principally in provincial centers such as Marseilles, Lyons and Caen.

All auctioneers are members of the auctioneers' syndicate, a corporate organization governed by law and having its roots in the medieval guild system. Syndicate members based in Paris conduct their sales at the Hotel Drout, an ancient establishment which contains many sales and storage rooms of varying sizes. Similar facilities are available to auctioneers in other areas of the country. The members also have separate business offices, but they are forbidden to conduct auctions outside the Hotel or other designated premises. Indeed, lawsuits are brought by the syndicate against its members if they try to break with tradition and hold sales elsewhere.

The auctioneers' syndicate serves as a professional organization for its members, providing them with administrative and technical services. In this respect it bears some resemblance to the National Auctioneers' Association active in the United States. However, the syndicate also serves as a sort of "communal" social security system. Each year, the members report their profits, and those making above a certain sum pay a percentage into a pool, which is then divided among their less successful brethren—a procedure unheard of in any other country.

The French system of buying and selling at auction also differs from that found in most other parts of Europe. French auctioneers, for example, are not allowed to buy and sell on their own account, but must deal only in consignments. Also, most houses don't maintain large staffs of experts, but rely on the professional advice of dealers and other recognized art and antiques authorities. These professionals work on a fee basis and are equally available to all members of the syndicate.

Consignments are obtained in much the same way they are in England and the United States—from estates, dealers and private parties. The auctioneers' commission is not fixed, but is subject to agreement between the parties. On the other hand, a standard buyers' premium is fixed by law. This is 16 percent on all purchases up to 6,000 francs; 11½ percent on those bringing between 6,000 and 20,000; and a flat 10 percent on all sales over 20,000. These rates are, of course, substantially in excess of what buyers in the United States must pay and are decidedly a factor to be considered in patronizing French sales.

Actual conduct of a French auction is similar to what you'll find elsewhere in the auction world. The auction season runs from mid-September to early July. Advertisements of impending sales appear regularly in major regional newspapers and in some popular magazines. They are, however, little more than listings of the lots to be offered, and are rarely illustrated. Exhibitions for major sales are held for a day or two prior to the auction; but for most auctions, the exhibition is confined to a few hours immediately prior to the sale.

You should also be aware that while there are a limited number of specialized auctions (old masters, silver and the like) for which illustrated catalogs are prepared, they are the exception. As a general rule, French sales are not by catalog. At the usual auction, you'll also find a wide variety of merchandise, both new and old. You may see a Louis XV sideboard sold directly after a television set, and just preceding a set of plastic cookware!

Bidding in France is conducted in much the same manner as in the United States and England. However, there seems to be a general lack of organization and concern for the buyer's comfort. Sales are held in tiny, crowded, overheated rooms with a high noise volume. The auctioneer picks up pieces, seemingly at random, and offers them to the public with only the most perfunctory description. Bidding is active and more or less frantic. As many bidders employ secret or hidden signs, it is often difficult to determine who is bidding or how much is being offered.

Particularly in light of the casual way in which many French auctions are conducted, you should carefully inspect the lots prior to sale. Also since French law, like that of most other European countries, gives the government the right to stop the export of objects regarded as of important national, artistic or historic value, you have further checking to do. While in the usual course, the government will notify the auctioneer at least two days prior to sale (the list of lots having been submitted some time before) if any of the consignments won't be eligible for export licenses, the responsibility of notifying bidders rests with the individual auctioneer. It is important, after attending the viewing at a French sale, and selecting the lots which you intend to bid upon, to seek out the auctioneer and specifically inquire as to the government position on those items. Remember, once the sale is over, it will be embarrassing—and quite possibly difficult—to obtain a refund on something which you find that you cannot take out of the country.

Happily, under French law all auction purchases are unconditionally guaranteed to be as represented. At any time within 30 years of the date of purchase, you may obtain a refund by establishing that the lot in question was not what it was described to be—a protection well in excess of that existing in other major auction centers.

In recent years, the French prohibition against auctions conducted by foreign nationals has led to the establishment of a flourishing auction center in Monte Carlo, capital of the tiny enclave of Monaco on the south coast of France. Although Monaco is protected, and largely controlled, by France, it has a certain amount of autonomy. This includes the right to allow sales conducted by noncitizens, providing they function through the intermediary known as the *huissier*.

The *huissier* countersigns contracts of consignment, arranges for the rental of an auction hall (typically the ballroom of a gambling house), and generally serves as a surrogate standing between the foreign corporation and the local government.

Using this device, such firms as Sotheby Parke Bernet and Christie's conduct several dozen auctions each year in Monaco. These sales are run exactly the way their New York and London sales are (though, of course, the franc is the medium of exchange), and often draw many of the same buyers. There is one distinct difference, though. While the bidding is handled by the house auctioneer, when the critical moment arrives it is not he, but the *huissier*, who brings down the hammer and declares the lot sold!

Of course, you'll find opportunities to spend your money elsewhere in Europe, as well. Switzerland has a substantial number of local houses in Zurich and Geneva; major English firms such as Sotheby's, Christie's, Phillips and Spink maintain offices there, too. The market is a rather specialized one, however, being centered primarily on very expensive items such as jewelry, old master and Impressionist paintings, French furniture and high quality antiquities. The nature of the clientele is reflected in the fact that foreign firms, as well as prestigious local houses such as Koller Gallery, hold auctions at the various ski resorts during the high season. Swiss auctions are conducted in the English manner and are most pleasant to attend, but can't be recommended for the auction buff of average financial means.

Holland has many fine galleries, both domestic and foreign, including Sotheby's, which bought a local firm in Amsterdam in 1979, and Phillips, which maintains offices in the Hague. Amsterdam, by the way, is outranked in Europe only by London and Paris as an antiques center. Early paintings, silver and clocks do especially well here. Auctions are held frequently, are well attended, and produce good quality merchandise.

Courtesy Sotheby Parke Bernet

"Modesta" by Diego Rivera: $130,000!

In Germany, Hamburg and Munich are the chief centers. As is the case in most of western Europe, outside of France, auctioneers are private entrepreneurs—regulated but not controlled —by the government. They are allowed to buy and sell on their own account, as well as on consignment, and set their own buying and selling commissions. Auction galleries are run—and sales are conducted—in much the same way as they are in England.

Austria has some auction houses, most of them concentrated in or around Vienna. Perhaps the most famous of these is the Dorotheum, which held over 2,700 auctions in 1978 and grossed $25.2 million. This vast number of sales reflects the fact that the Dorotheum, though known for its old masters sales, sells far more than antiques. Since the firm is part pawn shop/part bank/part credit union, it uses sales to dispose of unclaimed pawned items, household furnishings and the like.

With some 26 branches, the Dorotheum, founded in 1707 by Kaiser Joseph I, is the largest auction house in central Europe. Auctions are held every day, often two or three times in the same day; there are also several major book and art auctions each year. Knowledgeable auction enthusiasts maintain that the Dorotheum offers opportunities for good buys in a variety of categories.

Bidding is conducted in the English manner, but keep in mind that there is a 10 percent buyer's premium. There is also an 8 to 30 percent state sales tax, but this does not apply to lots bought for export and paid for in foreign currencies. Austria has regulations (similar to those of France), allowing the government to forbid the export of items deemed important artistically or historically.

This is also true of both Spain and Portugal. An English gallery conducting an auction in Spain recently discovered, to its shock, that the government would not allow a single lot to leave the country! Neither Spain nor Portugal is a major auction base, however; and sales, other than those conducted by international firms, are hard to locate.

Much of the same may be said of Italy. The loss, over the years, of so many masterpieces has led the government to prevent auction houses and antiques dealers from disposing of and removing art works.

Asia is another auction marketplace. In March, 1980, Christie's held the first public auction ever run in Tokyo. Under Japanese law, auctions are by invitation only, and traditionally the invitations have gone only to dealers. Christie's dealt with this problem by issuing several thousand invitations to the sale! Christie's employees opened the sale by explaining to their potential customers what their auction was and how it was run. The bidders learned fast, for sales totaled over $6 million!

If you are planning an "auction vacation," it makes sense to concentrate your efforts in England, France, Holland and Germany with, perhaps, a few side trips to other countries, but remember that no matter how similar the auction may appear on the surface, no two countries have identical auction rules. So, learn the rules of bidding, determine how currency regulations and export limitations may affect your purchasing and always, always attend the exhibition before buying! Of course, the ideal situation is to have a trustworthy local person go along with you—someone who is knowledgeable about the local auction scene. But, when the ideal is unattainable (as it so often is), a polite, friendly chat with a local antiques or furnishings merchant might do the trick. The idea is that local citizens often are "in the know"—and are therefore people *you* should get to know.

16 The Serious Game That Always Was

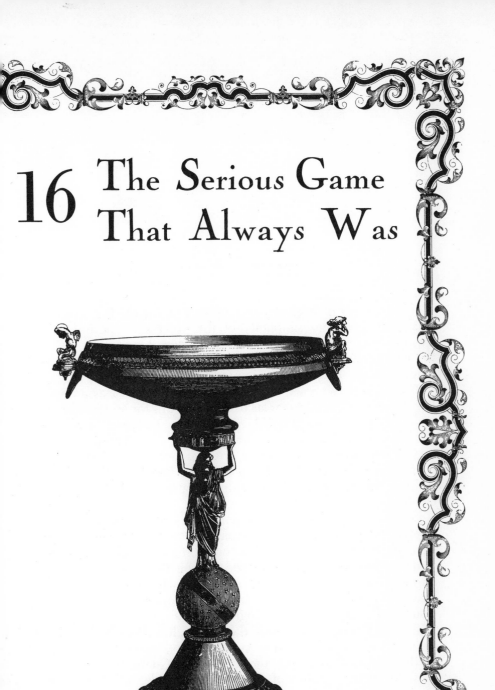

No one, of course, can ever be sure when the first auction was held. The very simplicity of the process (requiring only two or three people and an object), makes it quite likely that the auction exchange, as an extension of barter, has existed as long as people had surplus commodities.

The earliest reference to what we would think of as an auction appears in the Chronicles of the Greek historian Herodotus. He describes a sale, in fifth-century B.C. Babylon, of young women intended as "brides" for the purchasers. Though a system of advancing offers was involved and the term "bid" used, it remained for the Romans to coin the word auction, taking it from the Latin *auctio*, meaning, appropriately enough, to increase.

It appears to have been a common custom for victorious Roman troopers, having despoiled the bodies of their fallen enemies, to conduct an auction for those whose pickings were slim or who had, perhaps, arrived late on the scene. The overburdened warrior would plant a spear in the turf to mark the location of his hoard, and when his compatriots arrived, he would sell everything to the highest bidder.

To the Romans also goes the credit for the world's most extravagant auction. In the first century A.D., following the death of the Emperor Pertinax, the Praetorian Guard who had assumed effective control of Rome (and, incidentally, slain the Emperor), decided to auction off the entire Empire! Since Rome then controlled an area numbering in the thousands of square miles, and extending from Syria on the east to the British Isles in the west, this was no small "lot."

The announcement of the sale was greeted with outrage by

the Roman Senate and by the citizens, but since people who opposed the Guard had a way of ending up dead, the sale went off without interference. The victorious bidder was a wealthy Senator named Didius Juliannus. There is some doubt whether or not he really wanted the Empire; and, as it turned out, he, like so many subsequent auction-goers, bought a "lemon." For, Juliannus had been on the throne but a few weeks when the legions of General Septimus Serverus, who had learned of the auction, poured into the capital to set things right. The Praetorian Guard, in a fit of civic responsibility, killed the Emperor; the Empire was restored to the people (and eventually, of course, to Serverus).

Auctions, like most other forms of commercial exchange, largely vanished during Europe's Dark Ages; but, by the sixteenth century they began to reappear, stimulated in part by the new abundance of imports from exotic countries that were beginning to arrive in the seaports. The Dutch sold pottery, wine and even tulip bulbs at auction, but it was the English who really caught the auction fever. British auctioneers sold off everything from slaves to rare books in a trade so active that Henry VII (perhaps appropriately known as "the Huckster King") was besieged by merchants complaining that the sales were destroying their business. In response, he instituted some of the earliest laws governing auction sales, including the licensing of auctioneers and the payment of an annual fee based on the number of sales held.

It is hardly surprising, considering the strong Dutch and English influence in the colony, that New York became one of the earliest American auction centers. By 1676, less than 50 years after the city was founded, New York had a "vendee master" whose duty it was to supervise the conduct of sales and auctioneers. The fact that those who held this position had to post a bond of 200 pounds, a large sum in those days, indicates the importance of this position.

Other centers, such as Boston and Philadelphia, also had their auctioneers, but New York City remained the dominant center. By 1780, the New York City auction community had become firmly established, with members of the trade occupying space in the Merchants' Promenade or Auctioneers' Row, a group of buildings on downtown Water Street. From this time on, their advertisements appeared regularly in local newspapers.

Eighteenth and nineteenth century auction notices are shockingly similar to those of our own day both in the merchandise offered, which might range from real estate and fresh vegetables to used furniture, paintings, distressed merchandise and farm animals, and in the ways the sales were conducted. Notices, for example, spoke of the goods "being ready for examination" on a given day (the equivalent of our present-day exhibition), and referred to "catalogs" which were apparently quite similar to those presently issued by certain auction houses. Moreover, the term "without reserve" meant just what it does today, that the consignor had not fixed a limit below which the lot could not be sold.

There were some distinct differences, though. For one thing, early auctioneers would extend credit to their buyers for periods as long as six months, a custom so common that a discount was offered to those rare souls who actually paid cash! Another difference was in location. While some sales were held in "auction rooms" or at the sites where the goods were located, far more were conducted in the streets, on public wharves or even in coffee houses.

Moreover, auctioneers were more strictly regulated than they are today. There was a duty on auction sales as early as 1713, and in Manhattan, members of the profession were limited as to where and when they could conduct a sale, and were required to pay a yearly licensing fee consisting of a percentage of their receipts. Until as late as 1838, the number of people who could serve as auctioneers in New York State was limited by law. Despite these regulations, auctioneering was an extremely profitable business—so profitable in fact that in the first years of the nineteenth century some felt that it threatened the entire American economic system.

What happened is this: The War of 1812 coincided with the first real burst of English industrialism. Already, prior to the outbreak of hostilities, the British merchants were beginning to flood American markets with relatively inexpensive factory-made yard goods, pottery and glass. But, the war brought blockades and a general cessation of trade, particularly in the great port of New York. English merchantmen continued to ply the seas, but their stocks piled up, unsold in Canadian and West Indian harbors.

When the war ended in 1815, the ships descended on New York, Baltimore and Boston, their hulls bulging with cheap goods that had to be disposed of. The fastest way was by auction. The auctioneers, always an active but never a dominant

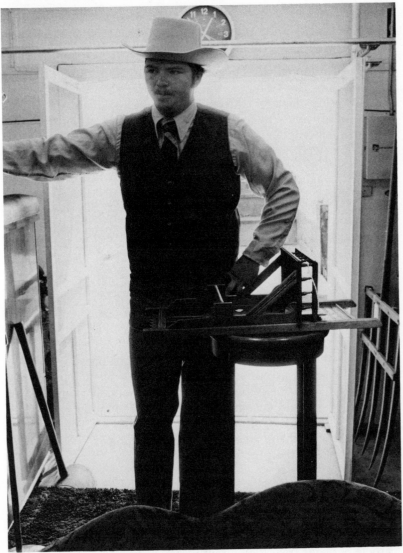

Courtesy Chun Y. Lai

Traditional style for many modern auctioneers.

part of the commercial scene, suddenly came to the fore. Two and three shiploads at a time were dumped on the wharves and auctioned off where they lay, at prices well below those being asked by American import merchants.

Business boomed at the auction houses, and all the old, alleged vices of the system came to the fore: shoddy goods, misrepresentation, lack of buyer recourse. The auctions became parties, of a sort, with food and drink for all in attendance. An American biographer of the period noted that the auctioneers were doing well, at least in part ". . . for they treat with good liquor liberally, and generally the bidders pay for it by paying for that which they bid up briskly."

During the greatest period of this auction activity (1816–1829), literally millions of dollars changed hands each year. In 1818 alone, it was estimated that $18 million worth of goods were sold in New York City, with auction proceeds in other ports totaling a further $12 million.

The effect on the economy of the infant nation was disastrous. The merchant importers went bankrupt by the hundreds, while new industries, potteries, glass works and mills, went under, unable to compete with less expensive and often better quality imports.

And, of course, the local businessmen fought back. It became apparent to some as early as 1813 that neither compassion nor patriotism would keep people from the auction marts. Only stringent laws could accomplish it. One of the many pamphlets put out by the anti-auction forces, "The Ruinous Tendency of Auctioneering and the Necessity of Restraining It" (New York, 1813), expressed the problem well:

> It will be in vain for government to trust to virtue of the people to resist the allurements held out to tempt them into the arena of some one of the numerous and increasing progeny of auction marts . . . If selling by auction were nothing more than a mode of sale, tending merely to change the disposal of any given article of goods from the present person in trade to other hands, it would be idle to make it a matter of serious complaint . . . but auctioneering is not a mode of trade; it is, in fact, a mode of destroying trade. It is a game at which none but knaves and fools can play, and in which the smallest portion of honesty is an inconvenient encumbrance.

Hard words, indeed; and you may be sure that the supporters of the auction system replied in kind. The battle raged all through the 1820s in the state legislatures and, finally, at the national level. Interestingly, little was accomplished. New York

Courtesy Chun Y. Lai

*The auctioneer and his staff.
Even at a small auction house
it takes close to 10 people to run
the firm and sales.*

An empty auction room awaiting today's assortment of bidders, buyers, bargain-hunters and more, who'll be playing "the serious game that always was!"

and some other states passed further laws regulating the field, as well as rules to reduce fraud, but the government in Washington took no action, primarily due to fear of angering Britain. Since many felt that we barely escaped with our skins in the War of 1812, they had no.desire for a rerun.

However, the problem gradually worked itself out as the British found other trade outlets and as American domestic manufacturers gradually were able to gain a foothold in their own market. The auction system ceased to be important in international trade and began to assume its more familiar rôle (to us, at least) as a redistributor of real estate and used household possessions.

Perhaps, the most spectacular example of this function to occur in the nineteenth century was the auctioning off of the buildings which were erected for the Philadelphia Centennial Exhibition of 1876. There were dozens of buildings on the grounds, and with the exception of the main structure, all were sold at auction. The structures had cost a total of $2.5 million, but they brought only $300,000 at auction. Those were days when you really could get a bargain!

The buying and selling of antiques at auction began to develop about this time. Furniture, rugs and valuable paintings had long been sold in this manner, but as furnishings, not memorabilia. In Europe, the auction scene had an especially early start. London, as discussed previously, was auctioning books in the late 1600s, and antiques in the late 1700s. France has had virtually the same auction laws since the reign of Louis XIV! However, around 1880, the first real American collectors began to appear. For years, these few wealthy men and women had the field to themselves, particularly as far as Americana was concerned. To most collectors, antiques meant Greek and Roman artifacts or, at most, Louis XV furniture and Italian paintings.

However, by the time of the First World War, the antiques auction was an accepted part of the American way of life. Sales were even used to raise money for charities such as the Red Cross; and some of the prices realized in antiques auctions during the early 1920s were not equalled again until the post-World War II boom. Now, of course, everyone is buying at auction, and the 1920s values pale in comparison with the figures recorded, not just at the big galleries, but at the smaller regional houses as well.

Auction! It's a serious game that always was . . . and from the looks of things, always will be . . .

Glossary

absentee bidding A form of bidding where the prospective buyer submits a written, or sometimes oral, statement as to the top figure he or she will pay for a given lot. It is left to the auctioneer or auction gallery staff to implement the bid at whatever figure within the authorization is necessary to gain the lot. In most cases, the bidder will not be present at the auction. Also known as *book, left* or *execution bids.*

agent In auction parlance, an individual through which a bidder acts if he or she wishes to remain anonymous or cannot for some reason attend the sale. The agent appears to be buying on his own behalf but is really acting for another, the true purchaser.

as is The *caveat emptor* or "buyer beware" phrase of the auction world. Everything at auction is sold "as is" in the sense that the buyer is responsible for examining and evaluating it for his own protection while (outside of clear falsehoods) the auctioneer is responsible for little he says or doesn't say about a piece.

auction A commercial sale wherein an object is offered to the highest of two or more bidders. The most important way in which an auction differs from the usual sale is that the prospective buyers, themselves, set the price through their actions rather than it being set by the seller.

auction block The podium or raised area on which the auctioneer stands while selling. The term is also used to signify the process of selling at auction, as "It was brought to the auction block."

auctioneer The individual who conducts an auction, directing the bidding and indicating completion of a specific sale with his or her cry of "sold."

bid An offer to buy made at auction, typically by raising one's hand, making some other sign, or calling out, "Bid!" or "Here!" Bids are customarily made in uniform increments, such as $5 or $10 amounts.

bidder The would-be purchaser who makes a bid at auction.

bidding The process of making bids on an auction lot which eventually culminates in the sale or withdrawal of the merchandise.

bidding limit A self-imposed sum which an experienced bidder sets as the top amount he or she will pay for any lot on the basis of its condition, market value and how much he wants it. Bidding limits are like diets. It is easier to establish one than to stick to it!

bidding number A number issued to each potential bidder at many auctions. It enables the auctioneer to identify bidders and their purchases. The number often appears on a *bidding paddle.*

bidding paddle   A wooden or cardboard paddle-like device, often bearing a printed number which is issued to potential bidders at some auctions. The bidder raises the paddle to indicate a bid or offer on a lot.

black light   A fluorescent lighting device which is useful in detecting additions and repairs to paintings, glass and ceramics. Restored or repaired areas look different under the light.

book bid   See *absentee bidding.*

box lot   A group of small items which may or may not be cataloged, and which are sold as a single lot, typically in a wooden or cardboard box. Box lots are generally "left-overs" of little value, though *salting* may increase their worth.

buy-back   An auction lot which has not reached its bidding reserve and is consequently not sold. Such items may simply be withdrawn or they may appear to have been sold to an absentee bidder.

catalog   A printed listing of the items to be offered at an auction. Typically, the items or lots will be numbered consecutively. At a more elaborate sale, they may also be briefly described, estimated as to value and, in some cases, illustrated.

catalog number   See *lot number.*

chargé   The right, in France, to conduct auctions. This right or license is owned by the state and sold to individual auctioneers.

choice, the   An auction phrase which indicates that a group of items is being offered, all of which are more or less alike (a set of side chairs, for example), and the successful bidder will be allowed to purchase one of the set for the figure he has bid. In most cases, the bidder will also have the right to buy each of the remaining items at the same per-unit figure. Also known as *the privilege.*

clerks   Auction house employees who record sales and bids, keep track of purchases, take payments, bid for absentees and perform other clerical functions for the gallery.

commission   The percentage of the gross selling price of a given lot (or all the lots from a specific consignor) which the auctioneer or auction gallery retains as payment for its efforts. Commissions vary from zero to as much as 30 percent and are negotiable.

consignment   One or more items which an owner has agreed to sell through a particular auction house for an agreed-upon commission and under certain conditions. Consignment arrangements are normally in writing.

consignor   An owner of goods who consigns them to an auction house or auctioneer.

counterfeit   In the auction business this term means an object which is not what the auctioneer specifically represented it to be. Since the auctioneer would never specifically misrepresent his goods, the term implies that he, too, has been duped. Many larger galleries provide for refunds where counterfeiting can be shown. To this extent, there is an exception to the usual *as is* policy.

deposit   A sum of money which the bidder must pay, either for the privilege of bidding or as a percentage of the price at which he has purchased given items at the auction. Unused deposits are, of course, returned. Their purpose is to discourage frivolous bidding.

desk, the   A term applied to the auction clerks as a group, particularly those who are executing absentee bids or relaying telephoned bids.

estate sale   An auction of merchandise from one or more private homes, typically coming on the market due to death of the owners. Auction buyers favor estate sales as the lots are "fresh," that is, they have not been offered for sale in some years.

estimate   The figure (seen as a range from high to low) at which auction house personnel anticipate a given lot will sell. Estimates are based on an examination of what similar examples have done at auction and private sale and are, by their very nature, "guestimates."

execution bid   See *absentee bidding.*

exhibition   The display, prior to auction, of lots which are to be sold at a specific time. Exhibitions offer the potential purchaser an opportunity to examine and evaluate those things on which he plans to bid.

fast knock   An auctioneer's technique to stimulate excitement in the audience, or to reward cooperative bidders. The auctioneer will ask for a low opening bid on a lot and will suddenly knock it down, without warning, to the first bidder. The fast knock is seldom employed after more than one bid is in as it would then anger others bidding on the piece. Also known as "deaf ear."

finder's fee   A sum of money, either flat fee or percentage of the

lot's selling price, awarded to those who provide an auctioneer with information regarding consignable merchandise.

floor This term refers to the area in which the auction is conducted, i.e., the "auction floor." It may also be used to indicate the reserve on a lot, i.e., the "floor" below which bids
will not be successful.

gallery An auction house.

handler An individual employed by the auction house to carry
things to the auctioneer's podium and to display them to
the prospective bidders.

huissier In Monaco, a government official responsible for assisting noncitizens in conducting auction sales.

layout An auction term referring to the sequence in which lots
to be sold are arranged. The ideal layout will not only
assure high prices for the better pieces, but will also enable
these to "pull up" prices on lesser examples.

leaders Choice auction items which will result in higher overall prices, both by attracting more people to the sale and
by enhancing with their presence all the lots in the auction.

left bid See *absentee bidding*.

lot One or a group of items (which do not need to be related
in any way) that are sold separately at an auction.

lot number The number assigned in the auction house catalog
to a specific lot of merchandise. This number should also
appear on the piece or pieces, usually by means of tag or
label. See also *catalog*.

mark The manufacturer's or maker's name or cipher which
may appear on items such as pottery or furniture offered at
auction. In general, presence of such a mark enhances a
lot's value.

opener The opening or first bid to be made on a lot at auction.
The auctioneer will often suggest a figure for an opening
bid, but will generally take reasonable lesser bids.

oral bid The usual bid from the floor made by voice or sign—
as opposed to written or absentee bids.

order bid See *absentee bidding*.

period A technical term to indicate that an object was made
during the stylistic period to which it is referred; for example, a "Queen Anne chair." See also *style*.

phantom bidder A nonexistent bidder in the guise of someone
in the audience, a *reserve*, or an *absentee bid*, and designed
to force legitimate bidders in effect, to raise their own bids.
This highly improper practice is indulged in by some few

auctioneers. It is hard to detect and even harder to prove.

pigeon Term sometimes used in the auction trade to refer to a prospective bidder who is easily induced to bid above his intended level.

premium, buyers' The percentage of the selling price charged as an additional auctioneer's commission payable by the purchaser. Long common in Europe, the buyers' premium has recently been introduced into the United States. See also *ten-ten system.*

preview See *exhibition.*

privilege, the See *choice.*

provenance The history of an antique, including: its maker, when made and where; by whom it has been owned; and when it was previously offered for sale or exhibited. Other things being equal, a good provenance (which is rare) will enhance the value of a piece to be sold.

puffing The customary exaggeration and hyperbole employed by auctioneers and other salesmen in promoting their goods. It is relied upon at one's peril.

pyramiding An unethical auctioneer's trick where false *absentee bids, reserves* and *phantom bidders* are employed in sequence to raise the bid several jumps between the legitimate bids.

resale number A number issued to dealers in furniture and antiques by state agencies, which enables the dealers to avoid paying the usual sales tax added on to the bid price (and maybe the buyer's premium, as well) at auctions. The holders of resale numbers are supposed to be actually in the business of selling antiques. Also, they may have to pay an annual fee and usually file state sales tax returns.

reserve The limit imposed by a consignor below which the auctioneer cannot sell his consignment. Reserves are designed to prevent pieces from selling for less than their true value. Most auction houses will not permit a reserve above the high estimate, and most fall somewhere around the low estimate.

rings Groups of dealers or rarely, collectors, who do not bid against each other at an auction and then later divide among themselves the lots which they have won as a group. The presence of a large and effective ring can depress auction prices.

runner An auction house employee who carries lots to successful bidders, runs errands for the auctioneer and may also relay bids to him from the audience.

running bids An improper auctioning practice whereby the prices at which lots are sold are raised or *run up* through use of various deceptive schemes. See also *phantom bidder, shill* and *pyramiding.*

run-up To induce a bidder to bid more than he intended, either by bidding against him (proper) or through subterfuges such as shills, fake absentee bids and the like (improper).

sale cost The "hidden costs" of an auction, often payable at least in part by the consignor. These include transportation and insurance for the lots and photography expenses where applicable.

sales tax A state or local tax levied as a percentage of the purchase price at auction and payable by the winning bidder. See also *resale number.*

salting The procedure whereby auctioneers put a good item into a *box lot* to encourage people to bid on what is essentially a bunch of junk. The term also refers to the habit of certain exhibition-goers of removing things they wish to bid on from one box lot to another.

secondary or re-auction An auction conducted by members of a bidding combine among themselves (see *rings*) at which they dispose of the items which they have successfully bid in.

shill An auction house employee who sits in the audience and bids against legitimate bidders, thus causing them to pay more for lots. An improper practice, but hard to prove.

sold The traditional phrase (often accompanied by the striking of a hammer on the table or podium) with which the auctioneer indicates that bidding is at an end and a lot has been won by the highest bidder.

spotters Auction house employees whose function it is to observe bids and to relay them to the auctioneer. The functions of spotter, runner and handler may often be interchangeable.

style A technical term indicating that a piece was not made in the stylistic period to which it refers but is, rather, an emulation of that style; for example, "Queen Anne style chair." See also *period.*

syndicate The organization to which all French auctioneers belong. It is part professional group and part a credit union or mutual aid society.

ten-ten system The European commission system recently introduced in the United States under which the auctioneer

takes a commission of 10 percent on the purchase price
from each buyer plus the commission which he receives for
selling from the consignor (which may also be 10 percent,
or more or less).

terms and conditions   The legal conditions under which an auction is conducted. These may include such things as warranties, form of payment accepted and when goods must
be removed from the premises. The terms and conditions
are normally posted in the area where the auction is conducted. They should be read.

track record   An auction term referring to how well the work
of a given artist or manufacturer or a given type of item
does at auction. Estimates are largely based on prior track
records.

vendue   The ancient European word for auction.

viewing   See *exhibition*.

warranty   A guarantee by the auction house as to the authenticity of a particular lot. Warranties, for the most part, are
limited to works of art; for example, a warranty authorizes
that a certain painting is a "Winslow Homer" and not from
the school of, or attributed to, Homer. Only a small portion
of the merchandise at most auctions is covered by a warranty.

withdrawn   The expression used by the auctioneer to indicate
that no further bidding will be allowed on a lot because the
opening bid was insufficient or because the lot did not elicit
the two or three bids required by house rules. Items may
also be withdrawn prior to sale due to damage or to such
things as problems with the consignor. Bidders may also use
the term to indicate (any time prior to utterance of the
word "sold") that they are withdrawing or canceling a bid
which they have made.

world record price   A term used to refer to the top auction
house price obtained for the works of a particular artist or
for a particular type of thing, such as a Tiffany lamp.
Achieving a world record price brings prestige and increased consignments to an auction gallery.

Appendix

Most people who attend auctions, and far too many who buy or sell through auction have only the haziest notion of the many forms used in the business. Even less is understood of the possible legal consequences implicit in using these forms.

Accordingly, reproduced on the following pages are examples of the most common forms used in auction houses so that you'll be able to recognize and understand them. Bear in mind, of course, that not all galleries use all these forms and some may use others. These, however, are the basic documents.

1. *The Auction Notice:* This official notice of an upcoming sale may be reproduced in newspapers or magazines or circulated as a flyer. Typically, it provides information as to the date, time and location of the sale and the terms upon which payment may be made. More elaborate examples may describe various items to be offered.

2. *Personal Property Auction Contract:* This is the contract through which an owner consigns merchandise to be sold at auction. It is a legally binding agreement but is subject to negotiation. Note the provisions requiring the consignor to pay for auction and advertising expenses and granting the auctioneer his or her commission on items withdrawn from sale within 60 days of auction. These are provisions for the seller to avoid, if possible!

3. *Consignment Check-In:* When the consigned merchandise is received at the auction house, it is recorded on the Consignment Check-In, and a copy is retained by both consignor and auctioneer. Be sure that all lots turned over to the house are recorded on the Check-In.

4. *Auction Lot Number:* Each lot to be sold at an auction bears a lot number tag similar to this. This number, which also appears on other auction documents, such as the Consignment Check-In sheet and the Cashier's Statement given to buyers, is the means of identifying individual items or groups of items as they pass through the auction house. Never remove this tag from the piece you are inspecting!

5. *Buyer Registration:* As each potential bidder enters the auction house, he or she is usually required to register and is given an identifying buyer's number. When a lot is sold, the winner's number is recorded by the clerk along with the lot number and the price paid.

6. *Purchase Notes:* Many auction galleries provide potential bidders with a sheet or card on which they can list the lot numbers and prices of items which they have bought. Such a card also lists the bidder's buyer number and, if large enough, may be held up to signify a bid.

7. *Clerking Sheet:* As the auction proceeds, the clerks sitting near the auctioneer keep a running list of each lot sold—its number, description, name or number of purchaser and price to be paid. In the event of a dispute as to what was sold, to whom or for how much, the house Terms and Conditions of Sale usually provide that this record is conclusive.

8. *Receipt or Clerking Ticket:* This receipt is prepared in triplicate. When an item is sold, one copy is given to the purchaser and whatever deposit he or she pays toward the knockdown price is recorded on it. When you settle your account with the cashier after the auction, the receipt establishes both your ownership of the lot and what remains to be paid for it.

9. *Cashier's Statement:* When you make final payment for items purchased at auction, always obtain a statement individually listing and describing by lot number, price and quantity each lot purchased. Without this receipt it will be difficult to get refunds or obtain other adjustments.

10. *Final Settlement:* This is the bottom line for both consignor and auctioneer, the point where both see if it was all worthwhile. The settlement lists the proceeds of the sale minus the expenses payable to the auctioneer and the auctioneer's commission. The remainder goes to the consignor. Note that, as consignor, you're obligated to provide good title, especially to things like houses and cars, and this obligation continues after final payment is made.

1

ANTIQUE AUCTION
THURSDAY, FRIDAY & SATURDAY
JANUARY 26th, 27th, 28th
THE INVENTORY OF:
HEIRLOOM ANTIQUES LTD., INC.
PLANT CITY, FLORIDA

TIME OF SALE: 1:30 P.M. to 5:00 P.M. and 7:30 P.M. 'til   — *ALL THREE DAYS*

PREVIEW: Merchandise on display Thursday from 10:00 A.M.

SALE LOCATION: 404 North Frontage Road, Plant City, Florida

DIRECTIONS TO SALE: Just off I-4 (Frontage Road runs alongside I-4) EASTBOUND (from Tampa) Exit 39, Cross SR 39 to N. Frontage, approximately ½ mile. WESTBOUND (from Orlando) Park St. exit, proceed to Frontage Road approximately 1 mile. (Across from Days Inn).

TERMS: Cash, personal checks accepted provided you have proper identification.

HIGGENBOTHAM REALTY & AUCTION CO.
Registered Florida Real Estate Broker
MEMBER
FLORIDA & NATIONAL
AUCTIONEERS ASSOCIATION
1702 Edgewood Drive, Lakeland, Florida 33803
(813) 688-6094

2

PERSONAL PROPERTY AUCTION CONTRACT

Agreement for Sale of Personal and Chattel Property by Auction

Agreement made this _____ _____ day of _____, 19_____ between

_____

of _____, hereafter called Seller,

and _____, hereafter called Auctioneers.

The auctioneer hereby agrees to use his professional skill, knowledge, and experience to the best advantage of both parties in preparing for and conducting the sale.

The seller hereby agrees to turn over and deliver to the auctioneers, to be sold at public auction the items listed below and on the reverse side and attached sheets. No item shall be sold or withdrawn from the sale prior to the auction except by mutual agreement between seller and auctioneer. If item is sold or withdrawn auctioneer shall receive full commission on the item.

_____

_____

_____

_____

_____

The auction is to be held at _____

on the _____ day of _____, 19_____ And in case of postponement because of inclement weather, said auction will take place on later date agreeable to both parties. It is mutually agreed that all said goods be sold to the highest bidder, with the exception of items specified by seller in writing to be protected. Auctioneer shall receive full commission on any item withdrawn from sale or transferred or sold within 60 days after the auction. It is further mutually agreed that the auctioneers may deduct their fee at set rate below from the gross sales receipts, resulting from said auction sale. The auctioneers agree to turn net proceeds from sale over to seller immediately following auction, along with sale records and receipts. The seller agrees that all expenses incurred for the advertisement, promotion, and of conducting said auction shall be first paid from the proceeds realized from said auction before the payment and satisfaction of any leins or encumbrances.

The seller covenants and agrees that he has good title and the right to sell, and said goods are free from all incumbrances except as follows: (if none **WRITE NONE**) _____

Item	Mortgage or Lein Holder	Address	Approximate Unpaid Balance

Seller agrees to provide merchantable title to all items sold and deliver title to purchasers. Seller agrees to hold harmless, the auctioneers against any claims of the nature referred to in this contract.

Seller agrees to pay all sale expenses including:

Auctioneer's Fee _____

Clerk's Fee _____

Cashier's Fee _____

Other Personnel_____

Advertising_____

Other_____

(x) _____   (x) _____
    (Auctioneer's Signature)   (Seller's Signature)   (Telephone)

                                                (x) _____
                                                    (Seller's Signature)   (Telephone)

PERSONAL PROPERTY CONTRACT — Form No. PPC-69 $2.00 per pad, 10 pads at $1.50 each, 20 or more at $1.25 each.
           Reorder from: MISSOURI AUCTION SCHOOL ■ 1600 Genesee ■ Kansas City, Mo. 64102

CONSIGNMENT
CHECK-IN   SELLER'S NAME_____Number_____

Street Address_____

City_____State_____Zip_____Phone_____

Other:_____

Lot No.	Description of Item Consigned	Quantity	Price Each	Total Price
1				
2				
3				
4				
5				
6				
7				
8				
9				
10				
11				
12				
13				
14				

TOTAL SALES $_____

SALE EXPENSE DEDUCTED _____

Received by:_____   CONSIGNOR'S NET CHECK _____

I commission you to sell the items listed above to the highest bidder by public auction. I certify that I am the owner of the above listed goods, merchandise, and/or property and have good title and the right to sell and that they are free from all incumbrances. I agree to accept all responsibility for providing merchantable title and for delivery of title to the purchaser. I agree to hold harmless the auctioneers against any claims of the nature referred to in this agreement.

Date_____

_____
(Seller's Signature)

DISTRIBUTION:
1. Original to auctioneer.
2. Copy to consignor at time of check-in.
3. Last copy mailed to consignor with payment check.

CONSIGNMENT CHECK-IN. Form No. CC1-69. $2.00 per pad. 10 pads at $1.50 each. 20 or more at $1.25 each.
Reorder from: MISSOURI AUCTION SCHOOL ■ 1600 Genesee ■ Kansas City, Mo. 64102

4

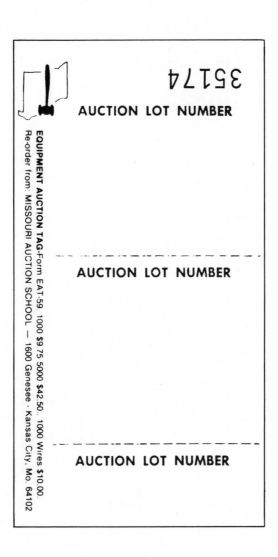

BUYER REGISTRATION

SALE FOR _____ DATE _____ PAGE NO. _____

5

Buyer's Number	Buyer's Name and Company	Street Number	City and State	Phone	Other

6

Your Buyer Number Is ▲

PURCHASE NOTES

Lot	Item	Price

All items must be settled for before
removing from premises.

7

 CLERKING SHEET

Sheet
Number_____

Sale for _____ Date_____

LOT NUMBER	DESCRIPTION	PURCHASER	QUANTITY	EACH	TOTAL	PAID

8

1

Buyer's Name
Or Number _____
Item or
Lot Number _____

_____ @ $_____   = $_____
REMARKS:

This receipt verifies payment and delivery of the above. Seller retains ownership until payment check is honored. Sold as is, where is. All sales final. Thank you.

● FORM NO. CT-12, MISSOURI AUCTION SCHOOL, K.C., MO. 64102

2

Buyer's Name
Or Number _____
Item or
Lot Number _____

_____ @ $_____   = $_____
REMARKS:

This receipt verifies payment and delivery of the above. Seller retains ownership until payment check is honored. Sold as is, where is. All sales final. Thank you.

● FORM NO. CT-12, MISSOURI AUCTION SCHOOL, K.C., MO. 64102

3

Buyer's Name
Or Number _____
Item or
Lot Number _____

_____ @ $_____   = $_____
REMARKS:

This receipt verifies payment and delivery of the above. Seller retains ownership until payment check is honored. Sold as is, where is. All sales final. Thank you.

● FORM NO. CT-12, MISSOURI AUCTION SCHOOL, K.C., MO. 64102

4

Buyer's Name
Or Number _____
Item or
Lot Number _____

_____ @ $_____   = $_____
REMARKS:

This receipt verifies payment and delivery of the above. Seller retains ownership until payment check is honored. Sold as is, where is. All sales final. Thank you.

● FORM NO. CT-12, MISSOURI AUCTION SCHOOL, K.C., MO. 64102

9

Purchaser_____

Address_____

City and State_____

Phone_____ Date_____

Cashier's
Statement

No._____

Sale No._____

Lot Number	Description	Quantity	Each	Total
	THANK YOU			

FINAL SETTLEMENT

Date_____

OWNER_____

Address_____

Date of Sale_____ ____Sale Location_____._____

Auctioneer_____Clerk_____Cashier_____

Other _____

PROCEEDS OF SALE: Cash.. $_____

                      Checks................................   _____

Other...   _____

....   _____

....   _____

Miscellaneous (see attached list)....................................   _____

                                      TOTAL PROCEEDS OF SALE...........................$_____

LESS SELLER'S SALE EXPENSE:

    Auctioneer's Fee .... $_____

    Other Seller's Expenses
    Advanced by Auctioneer:

    _____   _____

    _____   _____

    _____   _____

    _____   _____

    _____   _____

    Miscellaneous (see attached list)......................   _____

                              DEDUCT TOTAL SELLER'S SALE EXPENSE......$_____

                              TOTAL NET PROCEEDS TO SELLER......$_____

I, (or we), the seller of goods, merchandise, and/or property sold at public auction on above date and location, acknowledge and accept this settlement of proceeds of sale. I (or we) agree to accept all responsibility for providing merchantable title to all goods, merchandise, and/or property sold, and for delivery of title to the purchaser.

_____   _____
        (Date)   (Seller's Signature)

_____   _____
Auctioneer or Cashier's Signature   (Seller's Signature)

Index

absentee bid, 46, 55, 64-66, 69, 97-98
absentee bidding, 13
agents, 85, 111, 115
"American style" in painting, 28
Antiques Journal, 31
Antiques Magazine, 31
Antiques Monthly, 31
auctio, 162
auction block, 36

Barridoff Galleries, 104, 136
bidding limit, 25, 38, 52, 65
bidding paddle (*or* card), 53, 55, 72
bid up, 60, 70
Bilodeau, D., 13, 122, 125, 128
black light, 25, 91
"block," the, 121
book bid, 66
Bourne's, 19
box lot, 24-26
"buy back," 45, 101
buy-in, 95

Cassatt, Mary, 13
catalog, 18, 24, 26, 32, 36, 38, 40, 45, 55, 61, 64-65, 105, 108, 136-137, 144, 156, 164
estimate, 59
Charles Galleries, 20, 40, 46, 50, 66, 72, 125, 141-146
"choice," the (*or* the "privilege"), 61
Christie's, 18, 44, 46, 64, 92, 105, 121, 140, 149, 152, 157, 159-160

Christie's, warranty, 20
Church, Frederic, 7
consignment, 61, 86, 89, 98, 108, 114, 121, 133, 136-137, 140, 155
French, 156
consignor, 10, 14, 25, 46, 52, 85, 104-105, 107, 138, 140, 146, 164
counterfeit, 48-49, 76

"deaf ear," 58
Delaware University, 125
desk, the, 65-66
Dogpatch band toy, 11
Dorotheum, 159
Douglas Galleries, 140-141, 146
Doyle Galleries, 41, 44-45

"ending out," 22
estimate, 25-26, 137
execution bids, 46
exhibition, 18

fair market value, 11
fast knock, 58, 121
"floor," 69

Gregory Auction of Americana, 11

Henry Francis du Pont Winter-thur Museum, 125
Hobbies and Antiques Monthly, 105
huissier, 157

"Icebergs," 7
Indiana University, 125

191

International Auction School,
   The, 122

Jim Graham Auction School, 122
"jump bid," 58-59

"knock down," 97
Koller Gallery, 158

left bid (*also*: advance, order or
   sealed bid), 64-66
lot, 19, 38, 41, 46, 57-58, 60-61
   list, 36
   number, 26, 65
   withdrawal, 46

"mark," 58
Meissen, 28
Missouri Auction School, 122

National Auctioneer's Associa-
   tion, The, 119, 125, 128, 155
New Jersey Career Institute of
   Auctioneering, 125
Newtown Bee, 13
*New York-Pennsylvania Col-
   lector*, 31

Ohio Antiques Review, The, 13
opening bid, 55, 58, 66, 108, 144
oral bid, 53

"phantoms," 95-98
Phillips, Ammi, 28
Phillips Galleries, 18, 20, 64,
   140, 149-152, 157-158
"pigeons," 96
pyramiding, 93

receipts, 75

Repperts Auction School, 125
resale tax number, 48
reserve, 46, 57, 98, 100, 101,
   108, 152
reverse bid, 55
rings, 53, 55, 60-61, 111
runner, 53, 56, 73
run up, 37, 58, 96-97, 115

sale, advertisement, 32
   "by request," 144
sale, "on premises," 89
   terms and conditions, 40-41,
      48, 50, 56, 73, 92
"salting," 26
secondary auction, 60-61
shills, 92-93, 95, 98
Skinner's, 17
Sloan's, 105
Sotheby Parke Bernet, 11, 18,
   20, 41, 44, 46, 48, 66, 105,
   115, 121, 128, 130-138, 140,
   149, 157-158

ten-and-ten system, 50, 106-107
The Magazine Antiques, 105
Theriault Gallery, 104
toys, tin and iron, 11
Tri-State Trader Magazine, 31

underbidders, 16
Uniform Commercial Code, 41

Value Added Tax, 152

"Woman Bathing," 12
world auction record, 115
world record price, 16

Yale University, 125